POWER PLAYS
TERRY FARNSWORTH

TERRY FARNSWORTH

POWER PLAYS

THE EXECUTIVE JUNGLE SURVIVAL GUIDE

EBURY PRESS ₿ LONDON

Published by Ebury Press
Division of The National Magazine Company Ltd
Colquhoun House
27–37 Broadwick Street
London
W1V 1FR

First impression 1987

ISBN 0 85223 610 7

Edited by Suzanne Webber

Designed by Gwyn Lewis
Cover design – Harry Green

Filmset by Butler & Tanner Ltd,
Frome and London

Printed and bound in Great Britain by
Butler & Tanner Ltd, Frome and London

CONTENTS

CONTENTS

CONTENTS

PREFACE

Never before has business been so competitive. As companies struggle to survive in overcrowded markets the pressures upon profits become ever more intense. Cost-reduction programmes, efficiency drives, mergers and takeovers – all take their toll of executive jobs. Sometimes whole levels of management are wiped out overnight.

What will this book do for *you*? First, it will equip you with those vital political skills which you will need in order to *survive*. It will help to protect you against plots and stratagems and show you how to parry even the subtlest ploys.

Second, it will improve your *promotion* prospects. Here are those winning strategies that will make you stand out from the crowd and give you an edge in the promotion race. And – make no mistake – as firms reduce their management manpower, promotion opportunities will continue to shrink.

You will never be promoted unless you can survive. The surest way to survive is to be promotable. So why risk your future? Read this book.

PART ONE

ELEVEN RULES FOR EXECUTIVE SURVIVAL

CHAPTER ONE

HOW TO KEEP GOING WHEN THE GOING GETS ROUGH

– RULE –

Don't be discouraged by temporary setbacks – the only battles that matter are the ones you win.

Being a senior manager is like walking a tightrope: one false move and you could plunge to your doom. Management is no place to be if you are overly sensitive; to remain psychologically healthy you need the hide of a rhino. Make no mistake – there will be occasions when your hopes will be dashed, your feathers ruffled and your nose put brutally out of joint. You must learn to cope with these slings and arrows. Where there are roses you are bound to find thorns.

Every executive loses the occasional battle; it is part and parcel of a managerial apprenticeship. But what separates the craftsmen from the jobbing labourers is how they react to defeat.

THE MISSED PROMOTION

There is no sterner test of your mental resilience than being rejected for a job on which you set your heart. No matter how gently your ego may be massaged ('Don't worry', 'Cheer up', 'Your time will come'), the fact remains that it is someone else who has been chosen to occupy that much-prized chair. It is a time when life in your present job can seem like a prison sentence: the work is hard and the outlook bleak. But being 'locked in' by your company benefits, you feel that escape is out of the question.

This is precisely the moment to take a grip on yourself; no one loves a self-pitying 'loser'. Do the opposite of what your enemies may be expecting and appear to have taken defeat in your stride. Make a point of congratulating the successful candidate (such gestures cost nothing but can win you friends) and show by your every word and action that you fully recognise that the best person won. Such evidence of good sportsmanship is absolutely vital since it marks you out as a mature executive. And even though you may be inwardly seething, smile benignly whenever you meet your rival.

Along with your efforts on the diplomatic front, cultivate a more dynamic physical image. Buy a new suit or dress, change your hairstyle. Make sure that you walk with a light springy step as though you were seeking an inspiring new challenge. Never trudge around the office with hunched-up shoulders looking like a walking advertisement for your recent setback.

Throw yourself into your job as if you had just been appointed and bombard your boss mercilessly with new ideas. Fire off memoranda that brim with self-confidence and chair your meetings with added panache. Make it clear that far from being a broken reed, dis-appointment has given you a new lease of life. By appearing to have taken your 'defeat' so well you will have staked out your claim for the next time around.

THE CHEESEPARING INCREASE

One of the more absurd myths perpetuated by modern business is the idea that rewards are based solely upon merit: the better your performance, the more you will earn. It is an admirable concept – one which has comforted many a hard-pressed executive – but as with any opiate the effect wears off. Slowly, as his or her brain begins to clear, the executive realises that the commercial counterparts of Santa Claus often act in mysterious ways. Sometimes it is the slothful who receive the biggest presents while more deserving performers are shabbily treated.

So much for justice, but how should you react when it happens to *you*? The answer is – make a fuss. The louder the better. Tear into your boss's office like an angry dervish and make the walls tremble with the force of your fury. Pull no punches. Pound the table. Threaten to leave (if you are really *that* good). But never never accept your fate stoically. To do so is to signal that you can be pushed around.

Paradoxically, your anger will be secretly welcomed since it will be taken as proof that you are an out-and-out materialist. Despite all the verbiage about 'non-economic incentives', companies expect their executives to be money motivated and if you fail to react you may be thought unambitious. By giving full rein to your disappointment, you are merely behaving as you are expected to do: to turn the other cheek would be interpreted as weakness. Thus you need not fear that your outburst will be resented. You are simply confirming that you have fire in your belly.

THE DISASTROUS PRESENTATION

Every executive ought to be a competent speaker: words, not deeds, have made many a career. Nevertheless, even the most gifted performers have their occasional off days when nothing goes right and their eloquence fails them. Instead of scoring their customary triumph, they leave the platform amid an icy silence. It is a time that tests the steeliest nerves since such public failures are not easily forgotten.

Assuming that you are a practised speaker (and there are plenty of courses that can impart such skills), there is little point in bemoaning your fate: concentrate upon trying to retrieve the debacle. For example, when answering questions after your talk, treat every comment with attentive respect – never use sarcasm, however great the provocation. By dealing with even the most inane contribution as though it contained some profound business truth, you will not only win the audience's goodwill – you may even recapture the ground you have lost. But if you lose your temper, then expect no mercy. A rattled speaker is like a punch-drunk boxer. His opponents can pick him off at will.

Similarly, when discussing other items on the agenda, show that your loss of form was merely a fluke. Be generous in your praise of your colleagues' ideas and refrain from condemning any proposal outright. Your aim must be to repair your fences by generating the maximum amount of goodwill. By appearing to see merit in almost any idea you will build a reputation for far-sighted wisdom. And your own contributions are less likely to be attacked.

15

One swallow, it is said, does not make a summer nor need one bad speech destroy your prospects. It is no use sulking in your tent: get on with the game as though nothing had happened. In this way you will live to fight another day when, hopefully, the gods will be more amiably disposed. And nothing is likely to give them more pleasure than a person who can turn defeat into victory. Gods help those who help themselves. It is the weak who revel in their own misfortunes.

JEALOUS COLLEAGUES

There are those in business who are fated to spend their lives watching the carriages of the successful roll by. The majority bear no malice and get on with their lives but occasionally you will meet someone who is consumed by jealousy and would like nothing better than to see your star fade. It is particularly distressing when such a person is a colleague – especially if you both report to the same boss. You can never be quite sure what games are being played when you are not physically present to defend your interests.

Whether you can succeed in improving the relationship depends upon how secure your enemy is. If he or she is deeply insecure and feels taken for granted, it may be that some judicious flattery is needed, which will give the impression that you recognise 'talent'. Or it could be that you would profit by letting your rival win a few minor skirmishes – the kind of battles that you can afford to lose. The important thing is that you should appear to lose gracefully, that you should seem to be more vulnerable than you are. After all, there are few sights more comforting to a suburban tennis player than to watch a world champion make a poor stroke.

Infinitely more dangerous are those able performers who fear you as a rival in the promotion stakes. Their jealousy is more likely to be skilfully disguised than overtly hostile and they may even attempt to pose as your friends. Your only defence against these saboteurs is to treat them as you would a supposedly 'tame' tiger: keep your escape route clear and don't turn your back. It is not a question of whether they will decide to attack you – merely of waiting until they choose to pounce.

Don't trust them, don't confide in them and do your job superbly: these are the three golden rules. There is no way of beating them except to outperform them and to match their expertise in concealing their thoughts. For you can rest assured that your mistakes and indiscretions will quickly reach the ears of your boss – albeit, sometimes, by a roundabout route. Don't hesitate to turn their own weapons against them. It may eventually occur to them that they are up against a pro.

THE BOMBSHELL RESIGNATION

The more able your subordinates are, the more likely you are to lose them – either to another department or, worse still, to a competitor. In the latter case particularly, it can be extremely galling to train people from scratch only to have them snatched from you as they are nearing peak efficiency. To parody King Lear, how sharper than a serpent's tooth it is to have ungrateful subordinates! Ought there not to be a law against such base 'disloyalty'?

Certainly not. Who do you think you are? Are you saying that because you have taught someone virtually everything you know such a person is therefore bound to you like some feudal retainer? If so, then you have been working too hard and have temporarily lost your mental equilibrium. Too much 'getting and spending' hath laid waste your common sense.

Grow up. Think positively. Recognise that every fledgling is *supposed* to leave the nest and to fend for itself in the outside world. It is not necessarily a criticism of the way you have managed your high flyer that he or she should have seized the opportunity to make a first solo flight. True, the timing of the resignation may be horrendously inconvenient – but was there *ever* a convenient time to lose a good performer?

Face facts: neither outraged indignation nor 'being hurt' are likely to have the slightest effect. Lose with as good a grace as you can muster. Find out more about the job and what the prospects are and wish your pupil the success that he or she deserves. Do not be drawn into trying to dissuade the leaver from moving by making wild promises that you cannot hope to keep. You will only be storing up trouble for the future if you fail to deliver something that was never yours to give. After all, it is for the *individual* to decide: it is *his* or *her* career. Don't part in a blaze of mutual recriminations. Who knows? Some day such a person might like to come back.

17

THE EMASCULATED MASTER PLAN

One of the first things to recognise when you are a senior manager is that you are competing for resources with other ambitious people who are equally determined to get their own way. Inevitably this means that you will not always be successful in obtaining those things that you regard as essential and there will be many occasions when your spirits may droop. It is particularly frustrating to return from a meeting where your budgets have been slashed and your forecasts rejected. But it is no use becoming an incipient paranoiac; you may have lost a battle but not necessarily the war.

So conserve your ammunition and make every bullet count (in jargon terms, 'manage by objectives'). This may mean abandoning temporarily some of your high-risk projects and concentrating upon those with a proven track record. The more results you can squeeze from your depleted resources the more brightly your escutcheon will shine 'upstairs'. After all, it is always impressive to higher management to observe an executive who fights like a tiger. They are much more accustomed to watching managers capitulate when the promised reinforcements fail to arrive.

One caveat: make sure that your boss approves your new strategy or you may continue to be judged by your original brief. If you have had to prune your earlier objectives, make certain that he or she agrees with what you have done (if there is any risk of backsliding, obtain approval *in writing*). It is only prudent to protect yourself against later possible charges that you have failed to achieve your targets. Don't hand your enemies your head on a plate. Remember, it takes only a memo to make you fireproof.

Unhappily, there will be times when you will be so buffeted by misfortune that a plague of frogs would scarcely surprise you. In a matter of weeks, or even days, you could miss a promotion, have your budgets cut back, and lose your best performer to a hated competitor. You may begin to feel like some modern Job whose faith is being tested by the gods of business or that you are being punished for some monstrous sin. But if you can survive these traumas your future is bright. None but the brave deserve a boardroom chair.

CHAPTER TWO

HOW TO RECOGNISE A DEFECTIVE EXECUTIVE

– RULE –

Stay away from losers – executives are judged by the company they keep.

I f all executives were perfect how dull it would be – it is their faults and peccadilloes that give business its spice. Indeed there could scarcely be a more chilling fate than to work for a company of immaculate efficiency, staffed by robots from business schools with minicomputers where their hearts should be. Imagine a firm with no 'communications problems' or one where top management always did the right thing! How one would yearn for those good old days when the daily panic made the heart beat faster – a blessed relief from the boredom of routine!

Fortunately there is no sign of such a millennium, despite the efforts of those spoilsport professors for whom 'the effective executive' remains a cherished ideal. Far from turning us into bionic whizz kids, management training has been stopped in its tracks by our stubborn refusal to trade our humanity for the soulless delights of total efficiency. And right in the forefront of the fight against progress are those sturdy individualists, the 'Defective Executives' – people for whom training is a waste of time. Let us salute these freedom fighters! Our lives would be the poorer without their blundering.

WORKAHOLICS

These are persons for whom work is an aphrodisiac, a Kama Sutra of endless pleasures to be lovingly savoured by day and by night. Being totally devoid of aesthetic feelings, they prefer to pore over a balance sheet than to waste their time upon Brahms and Beethoven (whose names might suggest to them a firm of accountants). They are not concerned with the quality of life. They would rather compose a memo than a minuet.

There is no facet of their jobs that they find at all boring; they devour reports like shredding machines. Incapable of delegating and trusting no one, they trek through their work like desert nomads, surmounting each sand dune of triviality with a dogged persistence that is wondrous to behold. It would never occur to them to rest at an oasis; they normally lunch frugally at their desks. 'Time is money' is one of their favourite savings. They spend their lives racing against the clock.

It is no use trying to change Workaholics; they are perfectly content with all this drudgery and toil. Give them a column of figures, a mound of files, and they will beaver away like souls possessed, lost in a world of fascinating minutiae. They rarely surface long enough to think about their jobs and are unlikely to sire any creative breakthroughs. They are natural pack-horses, not Arab stallions. It is foolish to ask of them more than they can give.

AGONIZERS

Agonizers are people who find it difficult to make decisions: they are paralysed by the problem of having to choose. Usually the most liberal and well-intentioned of executives, their fertile brains generate so many alternative solutions that they find it agonizing to make up their minds. It is no use trying to pressure them into acting quickly. The more they are pushed, the more indecisive they become.

Agonizers spend much of their time at meetings, contributing frequently at inordinate length. Unless firmly controlled by a tough-minded chairperson, they can easily wreck the most well-planned meeting and drive their colleagues to the depths of despair. At running meetings themselves they are totally disastrous, being ever reluctant to take decisions. Their favourite weapon is to adjourn a discussion on the grounds that everyone needs 'more time to think'.

Yet disastrous though they are in a leadership role, Agonizers have one outstanding virtue: they are far more perceptive than most executives and are quick to see the pitfalls in an unsound proposal. But instead of using their insights constructively and nailing their colours to a particular mast, they immediately dash for the nearest fence, leaving their colleagues to fight it out. It is this trait, above all, which makes them unpopular. After all, it is one thing to capsize an already leaking boat, quite another to refuse to throw lifebelts to the crew.

GUNMEN

By temperament the opposite of the dilatory Agonizers, Gunmen are in their element in a blazing row. They hold strong views on almost any issue and have about as much subtlety as a runaway bulldozer. Argument for them is merely a matter of decibels, the victor the possessor of the strongest vocal chords. They believe that people need to be intimidated and that *any* decision is better than none at all.

Unhappily, being the worst of listeners, they invariably bite off more than they can chew and are totally at sea in any complex discussion. Unable to cope with any subtle nuances, they see all issues in black and white terms, like the tough-talking hero of a cowboy film. Their techniques of persuasion are direct and brutal – at the slightest opposition they fire from the hip. Fortunately they usually miss the target. Indeed it is doubtful if they know where it is.

Yet, for all their truculence, Gunmen are lightweights who rarely succeed in imposing their will – except in situations which they directly control. It is not simply their manners that arouse antagonism; their ideas are generally far too simplistic and would cause more problems than they would cure. Allies whose support can be the kiss of death, it is better on the whole to have them ranged against you if you are attempting to carry a proposal through. Such poor marksmen are hardly worth cultivating – by firing so wildly they could well hit *you*.

21

PACIFISTS

Basically nihilists with no strong convictions, Pacifists want merely to be left alone, to jog along peacefully until retirement. Having seen so many 'shooting stars' sputter and die, they have no ambition to reach the top and are quite content with things as they are. Believing that nothing really matters, they are bored by enthusiasts and miracle workers whom they see as a threat to their established routines. They cannot understand why people should become so heated over anything so mundane as 'a matter of principle'. 'Let sleeping dogs lie' is their favourite motto and they do their best to ensure that they do.

Given such a low-key philosophy, their notorious inertia is hardly surprising and the atmosphere in their departments is about as joyous as a morgue. So deadening, in fact, is their effect on their subordinates that they are constantly inundated with transfer requests from individuals who fear that they are destined to stagnate. They cheerfully agree to such requests since they see no point in 'unpleasant bickering'. While they are not particularly concerned about running a 'happy ship', the last thing they want is a mutinous crew.

Strangely enough, despite their lack of morale, Pacifists are often thought of as 'mature' and 'statesmanlike' since they rarely take part in office faction fights. Such neutrality, in fact, is the secret of their survival, for posing no threat to any group they are considered harmless and left in peace. Not for them the cut and thrust of company politics or the excitements of plotting a coup d'état. The nearest they ever come to sticking their necks out is when they buy someone a drink at the Christmas Dance.

HERMITS

Frequently found in research establishments, Hermits are usually so absorbed in their work that they have little time for making human contacts. Surfacing reluctantly at departmental meetings, they endure each discussion with ill-concealed impatience, like gundogs straining to be let off the leash. When asked to contribute, they do so tetchily, making no effort whatever to sell their ideas. They care not a fig if people find them confusing. They do not expect to be understood by 'amateurs'.

Such arrogance does not endear them to either their superiors or their colleagues and they are generally regarded as 'difficult to manage'. But since their abilities are not in question – indeed some of their ideas have been found to *work* – they enjoy the reputation of being brilliant eccentrics who ought not to be constrained by normal management disciplines. Not only do they often have the chairperson's ear, but they also feel free to bend it whenever they wish. Having such powerful friends at court, they meet little opposition despite their many foes.

Gurus, thinkers and *enfants terribles*, Hermits live the life of a protected species, fearing neither predators nor the poacher's gun. Given the mystique that surrounds their work, it is hardly surprising that they should give themselves airs and positively revel in their Cassandra-like role. As managers of people they are worse than abysmal and rule their departments with a rod of iron. But with such powerful friends what matter such trifles? Those who cannot 'shape up' can always leave – an option which many are not slow to seize.

DILETTANTES

Denizens both of large corporations and of long-established family concerns, Dilettantes are somewhat foppish characters to whom there is less than meets the eye. Like Hermits, they are generally well connected to some powerful chieftain at boardroom level, but the key to their survival is not their ability but the sheer good fortune of a judicious marriage. Of all the qualifications for a successful career, marrying into the boss's family remains by far the best. An MBA is certainly better than nothing but cannot compare with a honeymoon in Capri.

Long on charm but short on brains, Dilettantes merely pick at their work like a weight-conscious manager at a business lunch. Bored by detail and incapable of innovation, they drift around the office exuding bonhomie and constantly interrupting their more dedicated colleagues. They act, in effect, as high-level receptionists, welcoming VIPs at the local airport, booking them into suitable hotels and wining and dining them in expensive restaurants where the atmosphere is even more exotic than the food. Naturally all this junketing tends to take its toll and they are rarely noted for their sylphlike figures. But who cares if they are just a trifle overweight? Every court jester needs some protective padding.

HOTHEADS

All things are urgent to these impatient individuals; the most trivial issue a matter of life or death. Waving their arms to emphasize their views, they look for all the world like runaway dervishes who have somehow stumbled across a business meeting. Temperamentally incapable of 'playing it cool', Hotheads are the kind of people who would pick an argument at a funeral.

Their tendency to rant not only irritates their colleagues but hots up the temperature of every meeting they attend. Even the most mild-mannered managers are quickly offended by their habit of lecturing them as though they were dull-witted schoolchildren for whom remembering their own names would pose a serious challenge. Yet it is not that the Hotheads underestimate the intelligence of others: it is simply that they cannot contain their enthusiasm.

Being chronically poor listeners, they continually interrupt those who ask questions, giving them no chance whatever to get their points across. Tetchy and irritable with their opponents, they make no effort to win them over but merely raise their voice a few more decibels, hoping to intimidate them into agreement. If this does not work they will relapse into silence and fix their critics with a sullen glare. The fact that no one usually takes the slightest notice causes them inwardly to fume with rage. They cannot understand why they should be ignored – can't these fiddling Neros see that Rome is burning?

But diverse though their various foibles may be, all Defective Executives have one thing in common: they are completely unaware of their personal deficiencies. Each lives in a kind of mental fortress, surrounded by a moat of self-delusion, which forms a barrier against any influence that might disturb their private worlds. They all believe that their problems could be solved if only other people would behave more reasonably. They are the Unseeing Ones, the Self-Deceivers. When such persons oppose you then you *know* you must be right.

CHAPTER THREE

HOW TO PUNCTURE A PLOT
AND CONFOUND A CONSPIRACY

– RULE –

Look for the motive behind any
proposal – the hidden rocks can be
the most dangerous.

J ust as science has still to discover a sure-fire shark repellent, so there is no way of insuring yourself against business plots. For as long as you remain a senior executive you will have to contend with a variety of manoeuvres, some fairly crude, others more subtle, all of which will test your political skills and your ability to detect a potential assassin. It is not merely a question of being light on your feet: you must also know how to counter-punch effectively. There is small satisfaction in avoiding a knock-out if you continue to lose all your bouts on points.

To become an accomplished plot diviner you need only cling to one simple thought: what shall it profit he or she who approacheth me? For make no mistake – disinterested propositions are hard to come by in business and to analyse the proposal is often to discover the motive. For behind even the most innocuous-sounding idea could lurk a quagmire of devious machinations into which your ambitions could disappear without trace. That outstretched hand proffered in friendship could just as easily conceal a knife.

THE SPURIOUS SABBATICAL

Although well established in the groves of academe, the sabbatical is far less common in industry since it strikes at the heart of a great business myth: no really valuable executive can ever be spared. Thus thousands of acutely bored managers are doomed to stagnate in their air-conditioned offices like battery hens. They live in a company-dominated world which few new ideas ever penetrate.

Nevertheless, sabbaticals do sometimes occur but they are not always offered from the purest of motives. Far from being intended as spiritual refreshment, they are often designed to get rid of executives who would otherwise constitute tiresome roadblocks. After all, it is infin-itely easier to reorganise a department if one's most powerful opponent is out of the way.

Another common use of the Spurious Sabbatical is to push through a policy that has been hotly opposed by the executive who has now been removed from the scene. It is by no means unknown for a returning wanderer to find his or her authority eroded, budgets slashed and most of the staff 'redeployed' elsewhere. This is why so many 'sabbaticalised' managers keep in almost daily contact with their most trusted aides. Who knows what may be happening back at the ranch. The Apaches could be preparing their final assault!

Don't rush into accepting the offer of a sabbatical unless you feel certain that your defences are sound: you could be purchasing a ticket to corporate oblivion. If you are fighting any heavy political battles it could be a sign that you are close to winning. The sabbatical could be your opponents' last throw, a despairing attempt to stave off defeat. Having failed to conquer you on the field of battle, they are pinning their hopes on a Trojan Horse.

THE FAKE PROMOTION

If some modern Pavlov were to experiment with executives, he would use words, not bells, to elicit the right responses. And pride of place in his verbal armoury would undoubtedly go to 'promotion' and 'money' – words that cause the heart to beat faster and dreams to hover on the brink of reality. Ah, what sunlit vistas are conjured up by that beautiful brace of 'executive motivators'! A holiday for two in Portofino, a Louis Quinze chair in the master bedroom ...

Given its attractions as an executive aphrodisiac, it is hardly surprising that promotion should be used as a potent gambit in corporate power games. It does, after all, take a perceptive manager to see through the lure of a more resounding job title (fortified invariably by a salary increase) to the hidden realities of a job that leads nowhere – one in which he or she will be left to stagnate. And it is far from easy to convince some husbands and wives that to refuse such an offer is an act of statesmanship. It may seem to them that their partners have gone quietly mad.

Be that as it may, you would be wise to decline the offer of a drink from a well which you have reason to suspect may be poisoned. Watch out especially for any job that is new – it could be simply a Judas goat to inflame your appetite for innovation. Once you have accepted 'this exciting new challenge', the door of the cage could slam behind you and you could find yourself trapped in a meaningless job. Many executives have found to their horror that they have sold their prospects for a mess of promises. What seemed like an Aladdin's cave of opportunities has quickly turned into a prison cell.

The best way of detecting a Fake Promotion is to ask yourself who would gain if you were to accept. Who would take over your current job – a hated enemy or a dependable friend? Would you be reporting to someone who you know and trust or to a person renowned for devious politicking? Would you still be in the running for the major prizes or merely plunging into a promotion backwater? These are questions which you must ponder carefully. It is no use winning a string of victories if, like Napoleon, you end up being exiled for life.

THE PIFFLING PROJECT

If you are going to survive in the business jungle, you need many of the qualities of the experienced tracker – particularly the ability to spot a false trail. For despite the familiar-looking scenery and that intriguing spoor that you may just have noticed, it could well be that every subsequent step will simply result in your getting lost. The bones of many an over-confident executive lie in unmarked plots in promotion graveyards. When the trail divides you must take the right fork or you may never succeed in regaining camp.

27

One of the commonest mistakes of ambitious managers is to grasp at the shadow and lose the substance. In their eagerness to prove themselves human dynamos, they snap at every passing opportunity and hurl themselves into meaningless projects that have been carefully designed to get them out of the way. By joining a 'task force' with high-sounding objectives they hope to stand out from the humdrum herd when in fact they are entering a cul-de-sac. While they are happily engaged in spurious 'surveys' decisions are taken which they would have fiercely opposed.

Should you be offered a place on such a team, think carefully before you decide to accept. Is there a real job to be done or will you merely be fencing with ghosts? For not every 'challenge' is worth accepting nor does every 'problem' require a solution. Only if the MD is *personally* involved can you be sure that the project is completely above board. Such people have no interest in wasting their time or playing games for the benefit of their underlings. Such sideshows are strictly for the lesser breeds.

THE UNHOLY ALLIANCE

Adversity makes strange bedfellows and occasionally you will find yourself lining up with your enemies to fight some powerful external threat. This often happens in subsidiaries of American multinationals when local managements temporarily sink their differences to fight off some projected policy change which they consider would blunt their competitive edge. It is, to say the least, extremely intriguing to see lifelong enemies standing shoulder to shoulder like a platoon of pygmies trying to ward off a marauding elephant. The fact that such allies have so little in common only serves to underline the seriousness of the threat.

But for every major battle there are a thousand minor skirmishes and here you must remain very much on your guard. Remember, if you make a pact with someone you detest it is bound to crumble when it has achieved its objective. There is no need to disclose your innermost thoughts to an individual with whom your interests may temporarily coincide. Business alliances rarely last forever; they can be just as ephemeral as fashions in dress.

It may be that for the purpose of the moment you may need to share certain types of information that normally you keep under lock and key – confidential reports, market surveys and other material of that ilk. Make sure that you reveal only such data as is absolutely necessary for you to win the day; to be more generous could be dangerously foolish. After all, knowledge is power in business and there is no sense in squandering your most precious resource upon a person who may be one of your bitterest foes. Sufficient unto the day is the information thereof. Tomorrow you could be at each other's throats.

THE ENGINEERED INDISCRETION

If you can't hold your liquor then sign the pledge: your career is worth more than a few gin and tonics. There is no disgrace in being a moderate drinker and if you keep within your limits you can still have a good time. Only mountebanks exceed their capacity and deserve no sympathy should their tongues wag too freely. The chief concern of really top-flight executives is with what they achieve, not how much they drink.

Nevertheless, alcoholic gaffes are a relatively minor hazard; there are more subtle snares to be reckoned with. Chief among these is the Engineered Indiscretion, whereby you are trapped into saying more than you intended by someone who is out to queer your pitch. For example, if it is known that you hold strong views on, say, who is the best candidate to fill a promotion vacancy, your enemy may craftily seek your views on the merits of some of the other contenders. Naturally, if you are unwise enough to defame their abilities and to refer to them in scathing terms, your foe will quickly ensure that they are informed of your remarks – which means that their friends will also be told. Thus at one fell swoop he or she will have earned you the enmity of a number of people who are unlikely to cooperate when next you seek their help or advice. Needless to say, such Iagos will not involve themselves directly in any of these manoeuvres. Invariably they will use the services of notorious backbiters and gossips who can be relied upon to add a few touches of their own.

Likewise, be exceedingly careful before sounding off about any company policies to which you may be opposed – that sympathetic listener could be a snake in the grass. The stronger your personality and the sharper your tongue, the more vulnerable you are to the *agent provocateur*. Remember, trust is not a harlot; she is a lady of virtue. Her favours ought not to be scattered promiscuously but reserved for those who have proved their worth.

THE TEMPORARY TRUCE

Not every duel need be fought to the finish; the price of victory is sometimes too high. If by winning your case you offend all your colleagues – let alone your enemies in other departments – it is more than likely that you will find yourself isolated, an outcast from the corporate fold. You must know when to take and when to give, when to do battle and when to quit. Occasionally it may pay you to call a truce in the hope that the opposition will disintegrate.

Truces, of course, can cut both ways – it could be your opponents who make the first move. It may be that they feel they need a breathing space in which to rally their forces for a final fling or to obtain the support of a powerful third party. Or it could be that they are trying to negotiate a deal with one of your most loyal and trusted supporters. Whatever their reasons you should remain on your guard, for a truce is by no means a capitulation. It simply marks a temporary deadlock, a short-lived pause before hostilities are resumed.

Sometimes it will gradually become apparent that neither you nor your opponent can hope to win and that it would be better if you both agreed to bury the hatchet. By dint of a little mutual horse-trading ('you back my plan and I'll back yours') what may once have seemed like a war to the death may suddenly blossom into a full-scale peace. Such violent U-turns are fairly common in business since 'pragmatism' is a much-prized executive virtue. There is scant regard for the kind of person who sacrifices a career for the sake of principle. Such gestures may be all right for academic purists but *not* for people for whom power is the prize.

These then are some of the commoner ploys which may be used by your enemies to out-manoeuvre you politically and to undermine your prospects in the promotion race. No matter how strong your position or powerful your influence, *never* assume that you are completely fireproof. As long as you are known to be able and ambitious, you must expect to attract your share of envy and criticism. Remember, for every Caesar there is a potential Brutus. If you rest upon your laurels you may end up with a wreath.

30

CHAPTER FOUR

HOW TO AVOID
SELECTION FOUL-UPS

– RULE –

Never take chances when recruiting outsiders – if you have any doubts, do without.

No matter how effective you may be at developing your subordinates, there is bound to come a time when you will have to go to the marketplace to fill a vacancy in your management team. Having placed the advertisement and screened the replies, you will invariably be left with a short list of candidates, all of whom appear to be worth calling for interview. There is, after all, no substitute for a face-to-face discussion. You are recruiting a whole person, not a curriculum vitae.

But take care: selecting an outsider can be a perilous business and many a strange fish may swim into your net. Some of the more bizarre contenders can be swiftly disposed of, leaving you merely to ponder how they ever came to be employed. But there are others who are not always so easy to identify and even when identified are more difficult to assess.

ROLLING STONES

These are essentially executive gipsies: their caravans have rested in many companies but never long enough for them to achieve anything significant. Not surprisingly in view of their many job changes their records are litanies of unrelieved failure, a series of fiascos bordering upon farce. But at least they never block anyone's promotion prospects since they have little appetite for sustained hard work. As soon as they are pressurised to get results they fold their tents and seek pastures new.

Naturally they will bombard you with all sorts of reasons as to why their various jobs failed to work out. They will rend your heartstrings with tales of injustice, paint gruesome pictures of sadistic superiors and strain your credulity with bloodcurdling sagas of shop-floor shirkers and boardroom drones. Needless to say they will always portray themselves as executive dynamos surrounded by idiots. You may think it curious that they should have been so easily misled into repeatedly joining such deadbeat firms.

If you recruit such people then you have only yourself to blame when they quickly revert to their old feckless ways. Having not the slightest intention of ever concerning themselves with anything less than 'policy decisions', they spend most of their time criticising their colleagues and avoiding anything which they deem a chore. When their chronic indolence arouses resentment they react as though they were being victimised. They seem to think it grossly unfair that they should ever be expected to 'dirty their hands'. When reproached, they prefer to 'resign with dignity' than to carry out tasks that they consider beneath them.

MARKET RESEARCHERS

Not every applicant is a serious candidate: some are merely testing the market. Anxious to bring pressure upon their current employers for either promotion or a salary increase, they are hoping to use the offer of a job to accelerate their progress within their own companies. Armed with your offer they will then confront their bosses and point out how valuable their services are. Such tactics are often crowned with success, especially if the firms involved are competitors.

There is no need to allow yourself to be used in this way; such people are not at all difficult to detect. Their reasons for wanting to move are nearly always unconvincing and the more that you probe the more spurious they appear. For example, they are often fond of claiming that they are beginning to 'stagnate' when a glance at their records shows that this is far from the case. Similarly they will murmur about needing 'a new challenge' even though they may have been only recently promoted.

These people are the spoiled children of business, having been over-indulged by their various employers. Their heads have been turned by too many ill-advised promotions, their greed inflamed by excessive salary increases. Examine their records and you will find that they have been more than handsomely rewarded for their services – indeed, that they have been paid more for their 'potential' than for their actual achievements. Having managed to get themselves labelled as whizz kids, they have simply exploited their employers' gullibility.

BOSS HATERS

Personality clashes are, of course, very common in business and invariably it is the subordinate who is forced to leave. There are some people who just cannot stand each other and whose working relationship is a daily crucifixion. No amount of 'human relations training' can heal the scars on such troubled psyches. The time is past for any well-meant 'counselling'; the only remedy is mutual separation.

The fact remains that very few candidates for executive jobs will ever admit to have loathed their bosses: they feel that there is something shameful about such a confession. This, of course, is part of the price that we must pay for having insisted that executives learn to 'get along': those who fail to do so may consider themselves outcasts. This is why so many applicants talk airily about 'policy differences' rather than admit that they have had a row with the boss. To leave because of a disagreement over principles suggests a person of integrity; a 'clash of personalities' sounds prima donna-ish.

If you succeed in unearthing their real reasons for leaving, resist the impulse to think badly of them because of their failure to level with you earlier. They have merely been observing one of the great unwritten laws that govern these interviews: 'you should not speak ill of your present boss'. They know full well that to break this taboo could cause you to think of them as being 'difficult to manage' or as people who are lacking in personal loyalty. Whether this is true is for you to decide, but you should not mark them down for their attempts at concealment.

33

NAME-DROPPERS

Trailing clouds of reflected glory, the Name-Droppers are Walter

Mitty-like characters who yearn to be the confidants of the rich and the famous. Believing that you will be impressed by their celebrated 'contacts' – most of whom are purely fictitious – they behave at the interview as though they were introducing a shortened version of an all-star cabaret. They believe that fame and virtue are practically indistinguishable and that being unknown is a kind of disease.

Having little to offer except their elegant manners (although in fact they often hail from fairly humble backgrounds), they would much rather talk about their fake social lives than answer your questions on their work experience. Understandably enough since, truth to tell, their records are rarely more than mediocre. Being devout believers in the 'old boy (and girl) network' they regard working for a living as a tiresome bore. They see themselves as natural patricians providing 'leadership' to the uncivilised herd.

Do not waste your time on these arrogant poseurs; show them to the door with all possible speed. They are the sort of people who if introduced to a duke would claim later to have been invited to the ancestral home. Fantasists who are living in a bygone age, they are banking that you will fall for their personal 'charm' – and that you still believe in fairy tales.

WHIRLWINDS

You can always recognise these flamboyant types (who are nearly always men). They sweep into your office like human tornados, every muscle a-quiver with entrepreneurial flair. Having pumped your hand with quite uncalled-for vigour, they rest their briefcases upon their laps, fingers poised for a fast withdrawal. Sure enough, as soon as you begin to ask questions, the briefcases open and documents appear which they implore you to read through there and then. It is rather like operating a human computer: you pose a question and a report pops out.

Nevertheless, there is no mistaking their ability; unlike some candidates they really do *care*. Having set themselves the goal of reaching the top, they are under no illusions about the effort involved and will need no prodding to get results. While their missionary zeal may sometimes tend to grate on you, remember that to them their work is all important, not merely a way of passing the time. They have no other resources to fall back upon should anything sour their ambitious plans, no hobby or interest to act as a buffer. They have gambled everything upon winning the race and would be mortified at the thought of finishing second.

Never take on Whirlwinds (of either sex) unless you are sure that their duties will keep them fully stretched. Like many talented people, they are creatures of moods and will soon become despondent if not constantly challenged. Be prepared for them to have some spirited brushes with those of their colleagues who prefer a slower pace – especially as they rarely suffer fools gladly. But if you are ready to face up to the challenge of managing them, their white-hot enthusiasm could revitalise your group. Life with such persons may at times be exasperating but it is most unlikely that it will ever be dull.

CREEPERS

In complete contrast to the aggressive Whirlwinds, these are people whose deepest conviction is that no human being is impervious to flattery. Convinced that if they can succeed in massaging your ego their own glaring weaknesses may escape detection, they behave at interviews like medieval peasants who are seeking favours from their feudal lord. With their idiotic grins and fawning manners they would have made ideal footstools for some ill-tempered pharaoh. Their one useful asset is an ability to take punishment. They generally deserve all the brickbats they get.

Their favourite strategy at the interview is to encourage you to keep on talking about yourself. Sitting bolt-upright, they hang on every word like a first-year college student who has yet to discover his or her tutor's limitations. Occasionally, if they sense that you are about to wind down, they will inject an enthusiastic 'Do please go on!' in the hope that this will recharge your batteries. After the interview has come to an end you may suddenly realise that they have been interviewing *you*.

Persons of meagre talents and even less moral fibre, Creepers should be avoided like the plague. Ignore their flattery and explore their experience – you will find it a far from onerous task. All those high-sounding claims in their letters of application will dissolve like snowflakes in the morning sun and there will be precious little left to tax your decision-making ability. If you have need of such lightweights to feed your ego it is perhaps time that you found yourself a good psychiatrist.

35

VETERANS

Veterans are often more relaxed than you are: they have attended scores of selection interviews. Like Market Researchers they enjoy testing the market though they rarely have any ulterior motive. They just want a break from their daily routines and a civilised chat with interesting strangers. They are not particularly worried about being offered the job, being quite well thought of by their present employers.

Nevertheless, being professional interviewees, they take the trouble to do their homework. Before attending the interview they will have researched the appropriate business directories and acquired a useful knowledge of your company's operations. As avid readers of the financial journals they will certainly have noted the current share price and have read any stories about the firm's future plans. They will have at their fingertips all the right questions about the financial results and may even have obtained a copy of the annual report. Needless to say, their questions about the job will be equally shrewd. They will not be fobbed off by vague generalisations. They know the difference between facts and fantasy.

Make no mistake – Veterans are nearly always very competent performers who could well prove worthy of inclusion in your team. While lacking the creativity of the supercharged Whirlwinds, they are solidly professional managers and administrators who will quickly win the respect of their less experienced colleagues. Their main limitation is that they are a little lacking in drive and are best suited to a relatively easy-paced job rather than one that is constantly beset by crises. While they are unlikely to win any prizes for innovation, neither are they likely to let you down. If you are seeking a superstar then look elsewhere. But if you need a sheet-anchor to stabilise your group you could do a lot worse than recruit such a person.

After reflecting upon all these perils of the marketplace you may be tempted to throw in the towel and to settle for someone within the firm on the principle that it's safer to promote 'the devil you know'. But unless your job specification was so wildly ambitious that only geniuses could have applied with any degree of confidence, it is nearly always a mistake to accept a second-rate candidate in the hope that things will somehow turn out well. While miracles can still happen you ought not to expect them. Silk purses are one thing, sow's ears quite another.

CHAPTER FIVE

HOW TO HANDLE APPRAISAL INTERVIEWS

– RULE –

Learn to mix the rough with the smooth.

From time to time you will have to interview your subordinates and award bouquets and brickbats for their past performance. And however much you may dislike such a judicial role (only downright sadists seem actually to enjoy it), it is nevertheless a task which you must learn to do well if you are to build a reputation as a successful leader. Unfortunately, the whole field of appraisal interviewing is alive with booby traps for the unwary executive. Here are six of the most common approaches, all but one of which lead straight to disaster.

BLUE SKIES

This is a technique for bringing temporary happiness to individuals who may be worried about their future prospects. It is frequently employed to convince ambitious high flyers that they have a glittering future if they stay with the firm. It is also used for mollifying young graduates who are beginning to feel trapped in their mundane jobs.

Blue Skies is the favourite ploy of those cynical managers who care not a jot about their subordinates' careers but who care very much indeed for their own selfish interests. Anxious not to lose an outstanding performer, they paint dazzling vistas of what the future may hold while being careful not to make any definite commitments. Skilfully playing upon natural ambition, they seek to persuade that 'the sky's the limit'. If only he or she will hang on 'a little longer' they will surely be rewarded with a crock of gold.

What concerns such bosses is not their subordinates' careers but the disruption that would be caused if they were to leave. Knowing full well how difficult it would be to replace them – and being accustomed to stealing their best ideas – they will use any ploy, however unethical, to keep the geese who lay the golden eggs. While flattery and cajolery are their natural allies, they will not hesitate on occasion to resort to deception. 'That job you are after is just around the corner. Why give up now when it's within your reach?'

And so by a telling combination of flattery and half-truth, they succeed in persuading the would-be leaver to stay. Being totally concerned with their own short-term interests, they give little thought to anyone else's aspirations and even less to the fact that they have indulged in trickery. After all, the next appraisal interview is a long way off. By the time it arrives they could have been promoted themselves.

SCREWDRIVER

While Blue Skies is merely a confidence trick, Screwdriver involves an all-out assault upon the luckless individual who has been appraised. It is usually employed by autocratic bosses who pride themselves upon their 'no-nonsense' methods and whose approach to getting their points across is to repeat themselves – but in a louder voice. It is a technique that is tailor-made for executive bullies who confuse intimidation with forceful leadership. A sure-fire recipe for high staff turnover, it can be extremely damaging to a company's image.

From the moment appraisees enter the room, they are subjected to a barrage of insults and threats. Every fault is magnified a hundred-fold, the most trivial error sadistically explored. Should subordinates be rash enough to defend themselves, they will instantly be told not to interrupt and to learn to take their medicine straight. 'Don't waste my time with your piffling excuses. If you'd listened properly, you wouldn't have made mistakes.'

Needless to say, such barbaric treatment often leads to an emotional scene and to the speedy departure of the aggrieved subordinate. But not all employees are able to leave – they may be too old or too ordinary to get another job – and the outlook for such persons can be bleak indeed. Their only hope is that one day the tyrants may topple, the victims of breakdowns that they have brought upon themselves. Meanwhile they must endure their elephantine sarcasm and take what comfort they can from keeping their jobs.

Screwdriver is rarely found in large corporations, except in a handful of 'sudden death' companies ruled by psychopaths masquerading as chief executives. Unhappily, it is more common in small family-owned firms with a long tradition of almost feudal obedience to the every whim of the current master or mistress. There are *never* any circumstances when its use can be justified. Those who practise it are merely signalling their personal inadequacy.

BOMBE SURPRISE

Given a healthy relationship between superiors and subordinates, the appraisal interview should hold few surprises. After all, if communications are good and both individuals trust each other, there is no need for them to spend much time on the past – they can turn their attention to planning for the future. But what if such a Nirvana does not exist and the boss is jealous or suspicious of the subordinate? In this case it is more than likely that such a person will positively *revel* in exploding a Bombe Surprise.

The subordinate will be accused of 'falling down on the job' – a charge which comes as a nasty shock since no hint will have been received of the boss's displeasure. Sometimes, for example, subordinates may be blamed for neglecting a responsibility that they never even knew was theirs, or for working too long on 'trivial tasks'. Again, they may be charged with not using their authority or with taking decisions without the boss's approval. In short, no matter what they have accomplished, they will find themselves being criticised for their 'sins of omission'. Their protests, of course, will be swept aside. They will be told that they are lacking in common sense.

39

Such wrangles occur mainly in those Neanderthal companies that believe implicitly in 'the survival of the fittest'. Dismissing job descriptions as a 'bureaucratic fad' and management by objectives as a 'utopian illusion', such firms are natural breeding grounds for Bombe Surprise and a host of other Machiavellian practices. 'Keep 'em guessing' is the motto of these industrial dinosaurs since nothing must endanger 'the rights of management'. The resultant chaos is conveniently overlooked – as is the cost of replacing those who resign.

The use of Bombe Surprise can scarcely ever by justified, except when a person is suspected of gross dishonesty and is being given a chance to put his or her side of the case. If such people continue to lie without batting an eyelid, confront them with the evidence that you have previously gathered and dispense with their services as quickly as possible. For while a repentant sinner is potentially forgivable, a brazen cheater deserves no mercy. But apart from such cases, forget Bombe Surprise. It is a technique for spy catchers, not for ethical businessmen.

SMOKESCREEN

This technique is particularly favoured by those appraisers who dread having to hold appraisal interviews which they perceive as tending to 'rock the boat' and as worsening, rather than improving, personal relationships. For them the potential frankness of the appraisal interview is a lethal threat to their status as bosses. They would rather their subordinates were seen but not heard.

Nevertheless, being forced by company policy to hold such discussions, they are determined that they should be as painless as possible. Instead of allocating praise or blame (for such directness is anathema to them), they prefer to generate huge verbal smokescreeens of platitudes and innocuous generalities. It is thus virtually impossible for the individuals being interviewed to detect whether they have been performing well or badly. Not unnaturally, they tend to give themselves the benefit of the doubt. If the boss has not been critical why should *they* worry?

Unfortunately, such optimism is often far from justified and in fact they may be performing well below standard. Their bosses, however, dreading a confrontation, prefer not to wield the knife in public but to take action in stealthier, more devious ways. These generally take the form of frequent 'chats' with their own superiors, detailing the subordinate's many failings – failings of which the person is completely unaware. Sometimes this may result in a confidential report being sent to the watchdogs of the personnel department or, if the offender is senior enough, to the Managing Director or even the Chairman. Needless to say, during a business downturn, the unsuspecting subordinate becomes highly vulnerable. He or she is generally among the first to be sacked.

The only legitimate use of Smokescreen is when the persons being appraised are approaching retirement and are unlikely to be capable of improving their performance. There is little point in hounding such people since the older the leopard the more permanent his spots. Far better to accept them for what they are and not waste time in pointless criticism. Let them spend their last years at work grazing peacefully. Appraising such veterans is a bureaucratic irrelevance.

PSYCHO

Business is full of would-be psychiatrists who pride themselves upon their judgement of people ('I could tell he was useless as he came through the door'). Having picked up a smattering of psychological jargon from some horrendous potboiler read on the beach, they are forever classifying their luckless subordinates into 'introverts and extroverts', 'leaders and followers' and numerous other black and white categories.

The trouble is that some appraisal forms encourage such inanities by requiring appraisers to assess personal qualities such as 'initiative' and 'integrity' or 'leadership' and 'drive'. Instead of being asked to comment upon the individual's results, managers are virtually given carte blanche to display their prowess as amateur psychiatrists. Small wonder that companies which condone these practices end up by losing their most talented executives and are constantly forced to make use of headhunters. It is one thing to be accountable for one's results: quite another to be judged by the kind of hare-brained superior for whom one's every characteristic is deeply 'significant'.

Fortunately, Psycho is a fast-declining technique which is rapidly being replaced by more objective assessment methods that have little to do with personality traits and everything to do with business results. But however much firms strive for more enlightened approaches, there will always be managers who yearn for those 'good old days' when people were summed up in one minute flat. Such dinosaurs will not willingly give up their prejudices. The re-learning process would be far too painful.

SWEET AND SOUR

This can be a very effective technique and is easily the most accept-able in human terms. It consists of initially praising the subordinate for his achievements, then gently changing course to consider any weaknesses. (With some individuals the process may work better in reverse. Having first knocked them down, you then pick them up.)

The great advantage of Sweet and Sour is that it creates an impression of fairness and balance and defuses any emotional time-bombs. This can be especially useful when dealing with pugnacious types, renowned for their ability to swap verbal punches. Instead of the confrontation that they had been expecting, they find their achieve-ments being handsomely recognised – yet without a trace of unctuous flattery. Few individuals will fail to respond to such treatment. Even the most formidable man-eaters usually behave like lambs.

Any criticisms that you make – provided that they are made tact-fully – will be listened to as though they were holy writ. Naturally, they may not always be accepted *in toto* but there will be little danger of upsetting such people; their fangs will have been drawn by your earlier comments. Indeed, far from behaving like prima donnas, they may begin to press you for even 'franker' criticism. It is at this point that you should gracefully terminate the interview. There is no point in pushing your luck too far.

While this technique is particularly useful for handling 'difficult' subordinates, it is equally effective with less aggressive types. Essen-tially a form of psychological massage, it leaves the appraisee feeling fresh and invigorated and anxious to continue to earn your favour. It is certainly the least obnoxious of interviewing techniques and will cause you to be spoken of as 'firm but fair'. And this, after all, is praise indeed. Most bosses are considered to be woefully 'out of touch'.

Nonetheless, not even Sweet and Sour is a universal panacea: we are dealing with human beings, not with robots. Basically, all that can be said about the appraisal interview is that if you have a good relationship with your immediate subordinates – and are careful to foster two-way communication – then it ought not to be too great an ordeal. But in the final analysis you reap what you have sown, so be careful you are not hoist with your own petard. Remember, as you judge others, so will *you* be judged. Every appraisal is an appraisal of yourself.

CHAPTER SIX

HOW TO GET RID OF PEOPLE YOU CAN'T TRUST

– RULE –

Be ruthless with petty crooks – no cancer was ever halted by an appeal to reason.

Just as the most respectable families have their occasional black sheep, so even the best-run companies can be penetrated by tricksters who owe no loyalty except to themselves. Smooth-talking, ingratiating and incorrigibly deceitful, such people are incapable of 'playing it straight' and delight in weaving webs of deception into which their victims unwittingly fall. Convinced that they are cleverer than anyone else, they pay scant regard to normal business ethics which they see not as rules to be respected but as irritating obstacles to be circumvented. In short, they are the rotten apples in the company barrel. Once identified they must be dealt with swiftly for they are capable of inflicting enormous damage.

This, unhappily, is easier said than done, since they are extremely skilled at covering their tracks and it is never easy to bring them to book. Should you have such individuals working for you, it is no use relying upon verbal reprimands which are likely to have only a temporary effect. You must be prepared to fight fire with fire, to meet their deviousness with counter-deviousness. For however distasteful such a role may be, it is the only way that you can hope to unmask them.

ACCUMULATE EVIDENCE

As soon as you realise that you have a viper in your nest, start gathering evidence of his or her misdemeanours: it is no use just hoping that the problem will go away. By all means reprimand the culprit as each incident occurs but do not expect such action to be effective – it will simply cause them to lie low for a while. Even though they may know that they are under suspicion, their vanity will not allow them to admit defeat. Convinced that they are far more able than you, they will merely bide their time before striking again.

Con-men and Con-women come in all shapes and sizes from expense-account fiddlers to inveterate plotters who are constantly seeking to promote their own interests. Their one common characteristic is their utter selfishness, their belief that business is a kind of jungle in which only the slickest can hope to survive. They are particularly contemptuous of those with integrity, a quality which they associate with weaklings and fools. They see such people as lambs to be devoured, mere victims of the trust that they place in others.

So build up a dossier against these villains and keep it constantly up to date. If you give any reprimands, record them in writing and outline the facts that led to the incidents. The more clearly you can demonstrate a whole pattern of misconduct, the better your chances of getting rid of them. It is foolish – and dangerous – to rely upon your memory. Catalogue their roguery as it occurs.

HAVE THEM WATCHED

Since Con-people operate in so many cunning ways, it is extremely easy to lose track of them; you need all the help that you can possibly muster. Remember that you can *never* relax and to thwart their ploys you need the aid of your friends. By confiding in colleagues whom you can really trust, you multiply the power of your eyes and ears and make it more probable that their ploys will be detected. Such tactics, though devious, are absolutely vital. Without them they may succeed in 'slipping one through'.

The more widespread your network of 'undercover agents' the sooner you will hear when danger is threatening and be in a position to counterattack. For example, such a person may be trying to under-mine your reputation by slyly publicising your most trivial mistakes and subtly implying that you are past your best. The more quickly you hear of such flagrant disloyalty the earlier you can bring it to the attention of your boss. For make no mistake, your boss's role is crucial. At every step you must keep him or her informed.

As Con-people generally operate on several different fronts, you will need a number of these human 'listening posts' – friends whom you can trust to act discreetly. Their job is simply to keep you posted about any discussions that they have with your enemy, thus enabling you to detect a potential plot. By piecing together these secret reports you ought to be able to uncover his or her motives and take appropriate blocking action. There is no small satisfaction in watching the intriguer opening a cupboard and finding it bare.

Do not expect your allies to take direct action: they can provide the ammunition but you must fire it. You are paid to deal with such problems yourself, not to palm them off on to someone else. Resist the temptation to call your friends as witnesses until an issue arises that justifies such a step. Once you have revealed who your sources are they are unlikely to be of much use in the future.

SUPERVISE THEM CLOSELY

However strong your distaste for close supervision, you must make an exception of the wily Con-people or they will surely abuse any trust which you place in them. They thrive upon being left to their own devices since freedom to them is an opportunity to plunder – to pursue their own interests free from control. Make sure that you set them demanding objectives and institute regular progress checks. If you simply trust them to get on with the job you are giving them, in effect, a licence to cheat.

And cheat they will – in a score of underhand, devious ways. Many, for example, run their own businesses from the seclusion of their offices, secure in the knowledge that their bosses trust them. Often their mammoth telephone bills eventually betray them, but you should also look out for mysterious messages from callers who refuse to identify their companies. The chances are that these are fellow wheeler-dealers with whom the trickster has formed a business liaison. They will only speak directly to him or her and will merely request that their calls be returned.

Other types of behaviour that you should keep a close eye on include frequent short absences due to petty illnesses and long periods at the office when such people cannot be found. Far from being ill or attending a meeting, it is more than likely that they are arranging a deal from which they, not the company, will benefit financially. Be sure to make it clear that you have noticed these absences and question them closely when they give you their excuses. While refraining from calling them outright liars, you should certainly indicate that you have your suspicions.

Do not reproach yourself for displaying your mistrust; it may not cure them but it will make them more careful. Others will have noticed their strange behaviour and if you take no action you will be labelled as 'weak'. As the boss you are accountable for them during working hours and you have everything to lose by turning a blind eye. When the showdown comes it must be clear to everyone that you did your best to cramp their style.

BIDE YOUR TIME

Rest assured: sooner or later all Con-people go too far, over-confident of their ability to continue deceiving their superiors. As soon as you are sure that you have such individuals in your sights, be careful not to rush into premature action but bide your time until the moment is ripe. They are the slipperiest of customers who could talk their way out of a firing squad. If you move too soon you could give the game away and give them time to prepare their defences.

Carelessness is usually the cause of their downfall, the result of pressures that they have brought upon themselves. Leading as they do such complicated lives, they are bound eventually to make a mistake, enabling you to move in swiftly for the kill. Almost always this will involve some act of dishonesty (whether petty or large makes no real difference). You can be virtually certain that they have committed previous offences and once you start probing the evidence will mount.

Once again, be sure to *document* the evidence: you must be certain that it will really stick. Dates, times, places, names of witnesses – all must be checked and double checked in case some glaring error should let them off the hook. Remember that you are facing silver-tongued villains who will twist and wriggle like cornered snakes. If there is a weakness in your case they will spot it – and exploit it. An ounce of preparation is worth a ton of hindsight.

Playing cat-and-mouse games with crooked subordinates can impose massive strains upon your peace of mind and, unless you are careful, can affect your judgement. However certain you are of his or her misdemeanours, remain calm and objective until you are ready to act. After all, you are not pursuing a personal vendetta: you are trying to rid the company of an incorrigible rogue. Until the moment of truth arrives, such a person is entitled to the same courtesies as any other employee.

SPRING THE TRAP

Slowly but surely events will move to a climax: the mistake will be made that you have been waiting for. Whether it is a complex financial swindle or some characteristic piece of devious politicking, he or she will have crossed that final Rubicon from which there must be no possibility of return. If you bungle such a perfect opportunity all your shadowing and tracking will have been completely wasted. This is no time to draw back from the brink. The next mistake may be a long time a-coming.

When you are sure that your case is absolutely watertight, send for your quarry and confront him or her with the evidence (if the offence is grave enough to warrant possible criminal proceedings it may be safer to conduct the interview jointly with your boss or, better still, the company lawyer). You must, of course, give the accused person a chance to explain, no matter how convinced you are of his or her guilt. If necessary, take notes of the explanation and read them back to the offender to ensure that they are accurate.

Now it is *your* turn to deploy your evidence: do it calmly with the minimum of emotion. There is no point in letting your feelings take over and diluting your facts with personal abuse – the more clinical you are the more powerful your impact. So long as you have really done your homework and have blocked off every potential escape route, you can trust the evidence to speak for itself. You will soon know when you have broken through. The accused will fall unnaturally silent.

47

But not for long – such people are nothing if not resourceful. Realising that the trap is about to close, they will thresh around vigorously for some means of escape. Almost certainly they will try to rend your heartstrings by pointing to their long and 'loyal' service, their partners' 'poor health' and the consequences for their children. Once again, it is all too easy to allow your natural compassion to deflect you from doing what needs to be done. If you falter now at the final fence you will merely be storing up greater trouble for the future.

GET RID OF THEM

Stand firm: depending upon the gravity of the offence, either fire them or insist that they resign immediately. If you allow them to resign it becomes a matter of judgement as to whether you permit them to work out their notice – but it is nearly always better to pay them off and remove them from the scene as quickly as possible. After all, if they wander at will around their old departments, spinning hard-luck stories to their more gullible colleagues, they may saddle you, undeservedly, with a reputation for ruthlessness – as though you were some latter-day Genghis Khan. And such are the vagaries of human nature that there are always a few simpletons who will actually believe them. A quite avoidable infection will have been allowed to spread.

Identifying, tracking and disposing of Con-people is a miserable business but one which you must be prepared to see through to the end. It is no use hoping that they will reform their ways; deceit and double-dealing are their stock in trade. Give them enough rope and they will hang themselves: give them too much and they may well hang *you*. Misguided compassion will only prolong the agony. There is a time for pity and a time for the knife.

CHAPTER SEVEN

HOW TO FIELD THOSE AWKWARD QUESTIONS

– RULE –

There are no stupid questions, only stupid answers – the questioner, like the customer, is always right.

O pportunity knocks not once but many times for the rising executive, though occasionally such opportunities are fraught with peril. For example, you may be asked to give a presentation at an important conference or to enlighten your colleagues on a new management technique. In all such situations it is not merely a matter of getting your message across, you must also deal with those assorted missiles that may be thrown at you in the form of questions. Some, of course, will be virtually harmless, mere paper darts that are hardly worth ducking. Others, unhappily; can be much more lethal and, if handled clumsily, can shatter your credibility.

Yet, curiously enough, it is not so much the questions as the questioners themselves upon whom the experienced speaker focusses his attention. After all, if you can assess the calibre of the marksman you are facing, your prospects of survival will be considerably brighter since you can then devise the right countermeasures. Fortunately, this is not nearly as complex as it sounds. People who ask questions at conferences and seminars nearly always fit neatly into one of six types. The examples given here are all from the male sex. You will recognise their female counterparts when you meet them.

THE WANDERER

The difficulty with this laborious fellow is simply to grasp what his question is – and sometimes there may be precious little to grasp. Like some ancient general re-fighting a forgotten campaign, his main purpose is not to increase his knowledge but to impress his listeners with his vast experience, however irrelevant it turns out to be. Instead of asking a question he makes a speech, rambling self-indulgently down Memory Lane and seemingly oblivious to the chairman's glare. Indeed it would probably take a bullet to silence him, so enraptured is he with his own self-image.

But be gentle with this tired old warrior: he presents no threat, merely a challenge to your patience. After all, he is not so much looking for an answer to his question as for some kind of reassurance that he can still make a contribution. So suppress any feelings of irritation and gracefully award him the recognition that he craves. Flatter him with references to his 'valuable experience' and agree with a few of his more harmless platitudes. By doing so you will not only make an old man happy, you will impress the audience with your iron self-control. And he who shows that he can suffer fools gladly can scarcely be regarded as a fool himself.

THE ROUGHNECK

Here is a man who is after your blood, a professional intimidator of platform speakers who delights in erupting from the back of the room (thus ensuring that everyone turns in his direction). With his bucolic countenance and leonine roar, he is grimly determined to stir things up and, if possible, to reduce you to a quaking jelly who will gladly agree with everything he says. His favourite weapons are words like 'rubbish' and 'nonsense', coupled with scathing references to 'half-baked theories' and to those who would have difficulty in 'running a sweetshop'. In short, he is simply a rather squalid bully whose purpose is to cause you maximum embarrassment.

50

Now you may well be a very civilised person with a praiseworthy tendency to treat differing opinions with the courtesy and respect that they normally deserve. But unless you 'take your gloves off' to deal with the Roughneck you will be attempting to stop a charging rhino with only polite appeals to his better nature. Far better to fight fire with fire and to show him who is boss. And rest assured that the audience will be right behind you – they will be relishing the prospect of your counterattack.

Tell him first of all that you 'strongly disagree' with him, while 'bowing' to his experience in 'the confectionery trade' (it will be a long time before he talks of running sweetshops again). Dissect his arguments with clinical precision and expose them for the ragbag of prejudices that they are. Pour scorn upon his windy generalisations and establish your authority with well-chosen examples. Above all, make sure that your manner matches the ferocity of your attack. This is no time for chivalrously conceding points – you must aim to deliver a knock-out blow.

You will have no further trouble from this obnoxious know-all – he will be too busy convalescing to risk another encounter. And you will have shown not merely that you know your subject but that you also have reserves of moral courage, that you are no paper tiger to be easily brushed aside. This, of course, is a winning combination. Every audience loves a speaker who is not afraid of a fight.

THE EAGER BEAVER

This earnest seeker after truth can be one of your strongest allies and provides a welcome contrast to the thuggery of the Roughneck. Priding himself upon his willingness to learn, his questions can give you many useful opportunities to clarify points that may not be clear. Though he may at times appear somewhat critical, he is basically only seeking confirmation that he has correctly interpreted what he *thought* you said. Never dream of rebuking this harmless fellow. There is no merit in putting a mouse to flight.

The only problem that arises in handling the Beaver is to prevent him from monopolising the discussion period so that other members can get a word in. Unless you exercise some form of subtle control (assuming that the chairperson does not do it for you), you are likely to be swamped by a torrent of questions that may well send the rest of the audience to sleep. So without antagonising this likeable enthusiast, you must gently indicate when you have had enough. Thank him for his questions and suggest that 'we now move on' to hear from 'other experienced people'. Such a sop to his vanity will not only silence him but will leave him convinced that he has been the star of the show.

THE SHOW-OFF

Some people ask questions not because they seek answers but simply to indulge in a public preening session which they hope will dazzle the more impressionable onlookers. Invariably name-droppers of monumental proportions, they can scarcely utter a sentence without trying to convince you of their impeccable breeding and top-drawer connections. Every institution, however laudable, is bound to give birth to the occasional black sheep.

Sometimes the Show-Off is of the intellectual variety and will quote Vergil and Shakespeare in an attempt to humble you; at other times he will claim spurious political contacts. But do not be overawed by this pompous poseur, for despite his egomania he is highly deflatable. It is merely a question of cutting him down to size and of refusing to take part in his childish games. Simply answer his question as succinctly as possible and show by your manner that you are far from impressed. By being both blunt and brief you will deny him the opportunity for further exhibitionism and win the approval of the long-suffering audience. And it is most unlikely that he will intervene again. He is hardly the stuff of which heroes are made.

THE STANDARD BEARER

If you happen to speak frequently at management conferences you will find yourself recognising certain faces in the audience, even though their names may be completely unknown to you. These are the Standard Bearers, a curious breed of professional course-goers who are assigned by their companies to attend all manner of conferences in the hope of unearthing some new ideas. This, at least, is what they are told by their bosses but all too often it is no more than a half-truth. The reality is that they have been put out to grass.

Be merciful with these sad-faced wanderers for their lives are filled with aching boredom and a wistful yearning for early retirement. Yet, loyal troupers that they are, they will always come prepared with at least one 'burning question' which they have probably asked at a dozen other conferences as if trying to justify their expense account lunches. Not infrequently these questions are virtually unanswerable since they would require you to possess almost supernatural insights into the complex workings of the human psyche. A typical example is 'What motivates managers?'. Another old favourite is 'Are leaders born or made?'.

Still, there is plenty here for you to get your teeth into and no one will be expecting a definitive reply. You need do no more than skate around the edges of the topic, leaving ample scope for other would-be gurus to peddle their own particular management cure-alls. As for the Standard Bearer, it is highly improbable that you will hear from him again; after all, he knows all the arguments virtually by heart. He will have done his duty by asking the question. His eyes may stay open but he will be mentally asleep.

THE WEASEL

Here is a man for whom life is a perpetual courtroom drama with himself in the role of prosecuting counsel. Deeply unaware of his impact upon others, he sees himself as possessing outstanding legal talents, notably an unrivalled command of logic. Lurking in the audience like some pin-striped saboteur, he specialises in jotting down your actual words in the hope of later hoisting you with your own petard. While he is busy writing he is of course not *listening*, which invariably means that he misses the point.

Nevertheless, during question time, he will arise from his seat like an avenging fury and proceed to point out certain 'gaps' in your logic which he sneeringly implies demolish your case. Once again, you should not hesitate to deal roughly with this legal weasel, secure in the knowledge that you will have the audience's support. Tell him quite bluntly that if he had listened more carefully he would not have arrived at such erroneous conclusions. Recapitulate any points on which he has misquoted you and demonstrate unmistakably that the fault is his. As a *coup de grâce* (if he has been particularly offensive) you can enquire of the audience in general whether anyone else shares the Weasel's views. Rest assured: you will have no takers. His serpentine wiles will have alienated all.

One final point. If you are asked a question that utterly confounds you, never be afraid to admit that you are 'stumped'. Far from losing your credibility with the audience, you will be seen as someone with the kind of integrity that clearly distinguishes the professional from the charlatan. After all, no one expects you to have an answer for everything: only politicians still cling to such illusions. And we have long since lost our illusions about *them*.

CHAPTER EIGHT

HOW TO SURVIVE IN AN AMERICAN COMPANY

– RULE –

Think, look and sound like a winner –
success is America's favourite
aphrodisiac.

As a non-American employee of a US multinational your prospects of advancement are inevitably somewhat limited: Uncle Sam, like the Devil, tends to look after his own. True, you may rise to a senior position in the management of a subsidiary company or even to a job at corporate HQ. But to reach the inner citadel where policy is made – to be on the short-list for Chairman or President – your roots must lie deep in the American heartland, for only then will you be completely trusted. Like those barbarian mercenaries employed by Rome to fight its battles against other barbarians, your material needs will be well provided for. But do not expect to be acclaimed as Caesar. Such prizes are reserved for the folks back home.

However, there is still a great deal to play for and the bigger the company the greater the opportunities. To join the ranks of the dollar millionaires you need not have cut your teeth on blueberry pie or spent your formative years in ice cream parlours. You can sparkle brightly in the corporate diadem even though you may be outshone by more precious stones. It is all a question of convincing your masters that you can *think, feel and act like an American*. How can this be done? There are six main strategems for inspiring confidence.

ACHIEVE YOUR OBJECTIVES

Nothing is more revered in American companies than the ability to make money, for profit is seen as a virility symbol, a collective flexing of corporate muscle that demands attention and commands respect. Equally, no one is more shunned than a loss-making executive, for here is a person with a deadly infection which, unchecked, could undermine profits and growth and explode the myth of corporate invincibility. Achieve your targets and you will remain untouched, even if you behave like a medieval despot. But if your profits slip – and, worse still, keep on slipping – no excuses will save you from speedy retribution.

Yet success cannot always be measured by the 'bottom line' or most staff jobs would not exist (a favourite fantasy of many corporate hatchet men). How, then, can you compete with the marketing elite if fate has called you to be a humble personnel manager or a teller of half-truths in public relations? The answer is simple: you must know what situations you are being paid to *avoid* – and make damn sure that they never happen. For example, if you are an industrial relations expert in a non-unionised company, then at all costs the unions must be kept at bay. And if this means injecting a little pseudo-democracy into the company under the sacred banner of 'employee participation', then so be it. Better to endure some occasional sniping than to incur the risk of regular set piece battles.

To American companies track record is all and no marks are awarded to honest triers who fail. For deep in the American psyche there lies a profound conviction that success and righteousness are much the same thing. The good guys are those who succeed in their jobs, while failure is a reflection of some personal inadequacy. Similarly, bad luck is seen as something that afflicts only the unsuccessful. Budding senior executives recognise no such constraint as they purposefully clamber towards the topmost peak with all the confidence and sure-footedness of a mountain goat. It is a simple creed but nonetheless powerful: to err is unfortunate; to forgive, unwise.

RUN A TIGHT SHIP

There are few greater sins in American companies than to employ more people than you need; such incontinence is regarded as tantamount to sabotage. Indeed, under some of the sterner regimes even the temporary employment of an additional clerk will sometimes be debated by the higher echelons with all the earnestness accorded to the marketing plan. Verily, it is easier for a non-American to become a vice-president than for a department's head count to exceed the numbers forecast. All this is a form of organisational weight-watching, designed to stave off 'manpower flab' and to keep the company 'lean and hungry'.

The lesson is clear: *never* take on someone if you have the slightest doubt that he or she will be fully employed. If someone leaves, think twice – or even three times – before you seek a replacement, for great will be your reward if you can soldier on regardless. Nothing will indicate your potential more clearly than your ability to screw the same amount of work out of the people who remain: you will have demonstrated your mastery of 'management by attrition'. At the same time you must take care to show concern for the health of your staff since any unscheduled coronaries could damage your image. Be sure to encourage them to take plenty of exercise (so long as it does not interfere with their evening workloads). 'All things in moderation' should be your watchword. Especially as regards activities unconnected with work.

BE A GOOD TEAM PERSON

Americans are above all a sociable people with a built-in love of convivial gatherings – a throwback, no doubt, to those far-off days when frontiersmen gathered around lonely camp fires to tot up the day's tally of marauding Indians. Then, as now, there was much suspicion of 'mavericks' and 'loners', who were viewed as potentially subversive elements, owing no loyalty except to themselves. Men harnessed their interests to the common good and slapped each other's backs to keep up their spirits.

Today the camp fire has been replaced by the Christmas Dance and other manifestations of corporate togetherness. But the guiding principle is still the same. Don't hang back. Get involved. Keep your glass topped up (but stay well within your limit). And don't cudgel your brains trying to think up pungent witticisms: these are strictly the prerogative of the top brass. You may, incidentally, find them far more pungent than witty.

Similarly, do everything possible to involve your subordinates in

57

your decision-making. Summon them to meetings, ask for their opinions and then explain to them tactfully why you cannot agree. Persuade them to accept near-impossible assignments and, should they succeed, be sure to let your boss know how skilfully you are developing them. The point is that however much you may have to manipulate your people, it must always appear that they are responding *willingly*. This will mark you out at once as an excellent 'team player' – the very stuff of the American Dream.

DON'T BE A 'SMART ASS'

To be patently cleverer than your boss is a most heinous offence in American companies – especially if you are indiscreet enough to let it show. Such behaviour contravenes one of the most cherished beliefs of American businessmen: the bigger the name, the bigger the brain. Dare to outshine your boss at work or, worse still, on social occasions and in no time at all you will be dubbed a 'smart ass' and your promotion prospects will begin to cloud over. It is simply not worth taking the risk if you are hoping to end up in some highly paid sinecure with the right to travel on the company plane.

It is those off-duty moments that present the greatest danger – the more informal the setting, the greater the risk. Generally speaking, try to avoid any subject that may expose either your superior education or your more refined tastes, for hell hath no fury like a bamboozled boss. This means not only excluding from your vocabulary any foreign words (particularly Latin quotations), it also means avoiding virtually any cultural topic that could leave your boss feeling intellectually deprived. Having firmly slammed the door on Western civilisation, you can then get down to discussing those perenially safe subjects: sex, golf, and whoever's marriage has just broken up.

FLY THE FLAG

There is no more important event in an American company than the annual management conference; it is a tribal gathering with overtones of a pilgrimage to Lourdes. Its purpose is to motivate the hard-pressed troops to attempt even greater feats of commercial glory and also to pay homage to those company heroes who have achieved temporary sainthood by beating their targets. Speaker after speaker mounts the rostrum, each clutching a pile of well-thumbed transparencies with which to dazzle the respectful audience. The lights are dimmed, the overhead projector hums, and those sitting at the back compose themselves for sleep.

If you are scheduled to speak on such a momentous occasion, make sure that you do not fall into the trap of appearing to be on an 'ego trip': beat the company drum, *never* your own. By all means be contemptuous of competitive companies and exult in the success of your business strategies, but assign all the credit to the members of your team and resist the temptation to puff out your chest. Model yourself upon those self-effacing authors who apparently would never have written their books but for the incredible forbearance of their adoring wives/husbands. While no one will believe in your show of humility, you will have shown your respect for the unwritten rules.

Similarly, make copious use of the correct American code words: it is vital that you should appear to be culturally integrated. Open your speech by offering to '*share*' your experience; close it by threatening to '*beat the hell*' out of your competitors. Other magic words include '*aggressive*', '*innovative*' and, above all, POSITIVE. You can scarcely use this last word too often. It shows that you are the kind of optimist who always looks forward, pausing only occasionally to watch your back.

WELCOME THE NEW

It is a fallacy that all American companies are whirlpools of innovation; some are closer to those lumbering dinosaurs who were doomed to extinction by evolutionary change. Nevertheless, in stark contrast to many British companies, new ideas are at least likely to get a hearing, even if relatively few of them take root. The reason for the depressingly high mortality rate is that so many of the proposed schemes are patently absurd, especially those concerned with 'motivation' and 'leadership'. Yet such is the thirst for miracle cures and wonder drugs that 'cowboy' psychologists can have a field day, like robbers being handed the keys of a bank.

However, whatever your reservations, you must always appear to welcome new ideas since there is no greater sin than to be regarded as 'negative'. Treat any imported charlatans with profound respect and feign enthusiasm for their hare-brained projects (whether you actually *do* anything is a very different matter). The same applies to those tiresome annual rituals that culminate in the birth of a new 'incentive programme', designed to rejuvenate the toiling masses. Though you may have seen it all a dozen times before, be sure to acclaim the lusty new arrival. After all, poor thing, it may not have long to live before it is quietly laid to rest in some PR man's file.

Finally, remember that every American company is essentially a *religious* institution, possessing a deity (profit), a theology (growth), high priests (the directors) and even sacraments (the sales forecast). The most important requirement for success is *enthusiasm* – the kind of messianic zeal that in earlier times launched a thousand missions to heathen parts (today we talk of salespeople 'penetrating new markets'). Sustain your enthusiasm and you can cast out fear; lose it and the Inquisition may want to have a word with you.

CHAPTER NINE

HOW TO DEAL WITH DIFFICULT SUBORDINATES

– RULE –

Act like a king, not like a courtier – being too soft could cost you your throne.

Every experienced manager expects to encounter the occasional 'problem child' – it is part of the challenge of being a boss. For while the majority of subordinates aim to please their superiors, there are always a few mavericks in any organisation, many of whom can be extraordinarily difficult to manage. Some are aggressive and extrovert; others are relatively harmless bores who can test your patience to its uttermost limits. Collectively they form a kind of 'awkward squad'. Here are six of the more familiar types.

MONEY GRUBBERS

There is nothing shameful about wanting a good income, but for some individuals money is an addictive drug, producing an insatiable urge for constant 'fixes'. However generous their salary increases, however large their annual bonuses, such people are never satisfied; they regard themselves as permanently underpaid. Like nomads wandering the desert wastes, they drift uncaringly from company to company, ever willing to trade in their present jobs for the dubious incentive of an extra thousand pounds. Occasionally they may find a cool oasis where they may pitch their tents for a year or two. But longer than that they rarely stay. The call of the cash register is far too strong.

Money Grubbers are always on the alert for the chance to make additional money and are none too scrupulous about the methods they use. Some will inflate their expense accounts by sumptuously entertaining fictitious customers, others will engineer occasional kickbacks from small suppliers desperate for business. A favourite ploy of the more sophisticated operators is to invent for themselves a few nondescript tasks and then demand a new job evaluation because of their 'extra responsibilities'. And so great is the naivety of some salary administrators that such blatant opportunism often succeeds – and is subsequently rewarded with a 'promotion' increase. Thus while honest men toil, con-men thrive. The more bureaucratic the system the easier it is to beat.

Fortunately, most Money Grubbers are incapable of such high-powered trickery and content themselves with regaling their bosses with heartrending tales about their money problems. Many have over-extended themselves financially by acquiring a lifestyle beyond their means which they then expect their companies to pay for; others are natural profligates who give no thought to what tomorrow may bring. Whatever your instinctive sympathies for their plight, never encourage such people in their follies by sanctioning company loans to 'tide them over'. Like blackmailers they will be back for more. Soft touches, after all, do not grow on trees.

SHOP TALKERS

While Money Grubbers are basically petty crooks, Shop Talkers are merely crashing bores whose lives are empty apart from their work. Whatever the occasion, be it business or social, they drone away about the minutiae of their jobs with the obsessional fervour of true fanatics. It is hard to tell why they should be this way since they are generally employed on fairly mundane tasks. But having no interests outside their jobs, they clearly find them utterly absorbing.

Being totally insensitive to the feelings of others, Shop Talkers can be relied upon to cast a blight upon even the most lighthearted conversation. Whether the subject is golf or fashion, they will quickly intervene with lengthy reminiscences that have nothing to do with the current topic but which portray them, as always, as lone crusaders, battling gamely against inefficiency and waste. Once mounted upon such hobbyhorses they are virtually invincible and are quite impervious to attempts to change the subject. There is only one way to staunch the flow: plead an urgent meeting and leave.

But bores though they are, they are not without their uses. Being incorrigibly indiscreet and self-important, they will often disclose titbits of confidential information that can enable you to stay ahead of the pack. After all, a reliable informant is worth his or her weight in gold and any personal idiosyncracies are well worth tolerating. So do not reject these most tedious of raconteurs lest one day you find yourself dangerously exposed, adrift on a raft in mountainous seas. Business moves in mysterious ways. You need every scrap of insurance you can get.

Shop Talkers are essentially lonely people who long to be accepted as 'one of the crowd'. Always on the outside looking in, their very verbosity is a bar to intimacy since there is nothing more lethal than a garrulous confidant. Doomed forever to plough a solitary furrow, they cling to the one subject they feel confident in talking about: their jobs. People to be pitied rather than scorned, they rarely survive the shock of retirement.

PRIMA DONNAS

There is nothing quite so wearing as those managers who see themselves as the sun around which the earth revolves. Arrant know-alls and blazing egotists, they act as though the company were their personal property and their colleagues serfs who should pay them homage. Intolerant of everyone's foibles but their own, they stalk the office like marauding panthers, ever ready to pounce upon others' mistakes. They regard themselves as supremely gifted, though their brains are far blunter than their viperish tongues.

Prima Donnas need to be handled firmly – unchecked, they are a constant source of trouble. It is not only their arrogance which sparks resentment, their stupidity, too, can be awe-inspiring. The male of the species is the bane of secretaries, the despair of his underlings and the man most likely to cause a strike. His sense of humour is equally gauche. He has been known to make jokes about the chairman's wife.

There is only one way to quell these bumptious upstarts: give them a taste of their own bitter medicine. Every time that they step out of line, express your displeasure in biting terms and make it clear that they are under close surveillance. They will then either try to mend their ways or start looking for a job in another company. Whichever path they choose you will have won the battle and gained valuable prestige in the eyes of your subordinates.

Prima Donnas are little more than puffed-up bullfrogs whose aggression masks an inner insecurity. Realising that most people dislike having rows, they give full rein to their bullying instincts in the hope that they will be marked down as 'natural leaders'. To be sure their antics attract attention but *not* for any reasons which they would approve of. Such petty tyrants must be dealt with swiftly. The price of appeasing them can be far too high.

INNOCENTS

Usually, out of the mouths of babes and sucklings cometh not wisdom but balderdash. Innocents, poor *lumpen*, are political infants, people for whom righteousness always prevails, starry-eyed Alices in a booby-trapped Wonderland. Incapable of detecting human deviousness, they fall into every conceivable trap and emerge unshaken, their ideals intact. They become human punch-bags for those who delight in making mischief.

The tragedy is that they are natural enthusiasts who frequently generate some excellent ideas. But lacking the guile to present them effectively, they find themselves easily brushed aside by those who regard them as impractical theorists. This does not, of course, prevent their critics from filching any of their ideas that seem to have a good chance of success. Innocents, however, rarely complain: they are not the least interested in personal glory.

Innocents are generally found in service functions, in research laboratories and, occasionally, training. They get their satisfactions from creative work and do not take kindly to close supervision. Their loyalties are essentially to the job itself and to the professional standards that they have set themselves. Bored by the thought of selling their ideas, they believe that 'truth' should speak for itself.

If you have any Innocents among your subordinates, try to protect them as much as you can against those ravening wolves for whom change is anathema. Undoubtedly there will be times when they will try your patience for they are totally bereft of political footwork and can be relied upon to ignore any danger signals. But at least they are people who use their brains and are not content with things as they are. Like those tropical islanders who dive for pearls, they will sometimes emerge with a valuable gem.

RATTLESNAKES

Here are persons whom you can never trust because they owe no loyalty to anyone except themselves. Born manipulators and inveterate muckrakers, they seek to gain your confidence by passing themselves off as your stoutest allies, people who would die defending your interests. In reality they would do nothing of the kind. Were you to find yourself in serious trouble, they would lose no time in changing sides.

Rattlers can be recognised by two dominant characteristics; their use of flattery and sly insinuation. Oily, ingratiating and full of guile, they see you as a useful, high-level puppet who can be made to dance to any tune that they choose. Therefore they use bucketfuls of flattery to convince you that you are the ideal boss. They like to talk of 'our special relationship' and of how much they appreciate your 'wonderful support'.

As character assassins they are veritable Iagos, skilfully feeding you with poisonous gossip that they hope will provoke you into impetuous action. The objects of their venom are invariably colleagues whom they instinctively recognise as powerful competitors. By turning you against such persons they hope to boost their own promotion prospects. But they are careful never to accuse anyone directly. Innuendos and half-truths are their favourite weapons.

The key point to remember about Rattlers is that they are constitutionally incapable of being straightforward. There is always an 'angle' to everything they do. With such vipers at your back you can never relax for they will surely take advantage if you are ever off guard. The only solution is to make life such hell for them that they fold their tents and seek pastures new. You may find it distasteful to take such measures, but if you are too indulgent the poison will surely spread.

WINDBAGS

Windbags are people who believe in 'contributing' as frequently as possible to every discussion. They are deeply in love with the sound of their own voices. No matter how ignorant they may be of a subject, they deem it their duty to make their views known since they see themselves as elder statesmen whose utterances unfailingly vibrate with wisdom. Once in full cry they are virtually unstoppable and can only be halted by the toughest of chairmen. They are the kind of individuals who would scarcely notice if they found themselves addressing an empty room.

Time means nothing to these ponderous wordsmiths and any meeting they attend is bound to drag on. Their store of clichés is like a bottomless pit, a water-hole that never runs dry. They are masters of repetition, sprayers of platitudes and dead-shots at making obvious points. Had they taken up politics they would have been in their element when opening bridges and village fetes.

It is no use being soft with these tiresome bores, their arrant verbosity must be firmly curbed. Make it clear to such individuals before the meeting that every speaker must keep to the point and that any offenders will receive short shrift. If they choose to ignore this initial warning then question them aggressively whenever they speak, making it obvious that you will not tolerate irrevelance. They will probably collapse like pricked balloons, thus allowing the meeting to achieve its objectives.

Do not fear that by handling them roughly you will lose the goodwill of others at the meeting, the Windbag is no candidate for a martyr's robes. Many of those present will have painful memories of time-wasting 'contributions' at previous meetings and will heartily approve of your forceful chairmanship. Far from being regarded as a cruel tyrant, you will be seen as a public benefactor, a modern Saint George who has slain the dragon. It is not often that you will find yourself so wildly popular. Savour the moment to the full.

Dealing with maverick subordinates such as these requires the skill and courage of a successful lion-tamer: in essence it becomes a battle of wills. But exhausting and irritating though the task may be, there is no surer way of preparing yourself for those boardroom tussles that may lie ahead – where the penalty for failure can be swift and deadly. Instead of resenting your 'awkward squad', look upon them as sparring partners with whom you must practise if you are to win the championship. Better the occasional bloody nose in a training bout than a first-round knockout in a title fight.

CHAPTER TEN

HOW TO AVOID BEING SET UP

– RULE –

Sleep on any offer, however tempting – Venus flytraps don't give second chances.

I t may be true that opportunity knocks but once, but some 'opportunities' are not worth having. Some indeed are mere subterfuges, cunningly designed to cosset your ego while subtly diluting your power or your influence. And all too often such ploys succeed. Vanity is the executive's Achilles heel.

So be on your guard against Greeks bearing gifts: you are most unlikely to receive something for nothing. However tempting the offer may be, examine it carefully before you accept lest you find yourself eating a poisoned apple. It is no use bemoaning your gulli-bility when your wings have been clipped and your position under-mined. A shipwrecked sailor has no bargaining power and may have the greatest difficulty in attracting attention.

The question to ask yourself is a simple one: if I accept this offer who else will benefit? Don't allow yourself to be dazzled by the surface glitter of a larger office or a bigger car – the road to oblivion is paved with such baubles. What really matters is whether the *job* is bigger and whether your *authority* will be increased. The title of the job may be utterly misleading. Who wants to rule over a managerial desert?

SIDEWAYS MOVES

If you are offered a job that involves not promotion but merely a chance to 'broaden your experience', then the question arises: what price the experience? It may well be that in a large corporation such 'job rotation' has long been established as a tool for developing future top executives, those jacks of all trades and masters of few. Or it could be that such moves have a motivational purpose, for example to put fresh heart into stagnating executives who have languished too long in their present jobs. But a third explanation is equally likely: an attempt is being made to ease you out of your job so that some rival faction can increase its influence.

The only way to detect such a gambit is to consider carefully what has happened to others who in the past have accepted similar offers. Where are they now, those once bright-eyed young hopefuls – perched at the top of the company tree or rotting away in some distant outpost? Did their careers receive an impetus upwards or did they begin to slide into corporate obscurity, their names forgotten and their promise quenched? If *none* of these people has made the grade then you should fight like fury to stay where you are.

The only exception to this general rule is where the person you would be working for is a company 'star', clearly destined for the commanding heights. Such individuals are unlikely to vegetate and will be looking for people who can promote their interests. Should he or she offer you a job, accept it at once. They will not be backward in showing their gratitude. As they scale each peak they will pull you up behind them and you could soon find yourself close to the top of the mountain.

TASK FORCES

If you are offered a place in a company 'task force', think carefully or you may repent at leisure. Assess whether the project is really needed and, more important, whether it can hope to succeed. It is one thing to be a member of a victorious army, quite another to be part of a defeated rabble. You cannot afford to be associated with failure. Gallant losers in business are a most prolific species.

Once again, the problem is: how do you spot a potential winner? So many companies are vulnerable to project 'fads', enthusiastically peddled by management theorists, that have little chance of proving successful. For example, if the MD 'sees the light' while on a business school course and is converted to the idea of 'participative management' or other 'enlightened' executive practices, a task force may be formed to usher in the millennium. But if he or she continues to operate like a rock-ribbed autocrat it is highly improbable that anything will change. The task force will be wasting its time and energies.

The best kind of assignment to be associated with is one where the results are easily *measurable* and do not depend upon managers changing their style. True, your failures become more visible but so do your successes. Better still, the effects are usually far longer lasting. After all, many managers are adept at changing their behaviour temporarily but when 'the heat is off' they quickly revert to type.

Another pointer to the team's chances of success is the calibre of the people who are recruited to it. If only top-drawer performers are being chosen, then clearly the company is deadly serious and is gambling heavily upon the expected benefits. But if mediocrities and misfits are assigned to the project, you can be virtually certain that it is only a charade. Reject any suggestion that you should join such a group. The kind of cheese found in mousetraps is best left alone.

OVERSEAS POSTINGS

You may have always wanted to see the world but overseas postings should be treated with caution. The romance of travel will quickly wear off when you find yourself living in some squalid hell-hole with an unhappy partner who is homesick. And even if you are posted to a pleasant spot with tax advantages and an equable climate, you may still lose out in the longer term. You could easily become a forgotten legionnaire with little hope of ever regaining your base.

As always, look for any hidden motives behind such an offer and ask yourself why *you* should have been selected. Is it because you already know the country and can speak the language with reasonable fluency? Or perhaps you have skills that are vitally needed to exploit the potential of a burgeoning market? In short, what makes *you* so special in this particular situation – why not others who appear to be equally well qualified? If you can answer such a question honestly and objectively (wishful thinking will only blur the issue) then by all means pack your bags and go. You could do your career a power of good.

But of course, to strike a more sinister note, the offer could simply be an ingenious ploy to remove you from your current position – to sidetrack you in the promotion race. Once installed in your foreign bastion, albeit surrounded by the trappings of affluence, you could begin to find your authority eroded as a result of changes at the corporate head office. Instead of operating like a feudal lord or lady ('you'll have a completely free hand, of course') you could rapidly become a mere 'country cousin' doomed to languish under alien skies. So be careful not to accept too quickly. Travel may broaden the mind but it could destroy your prospects.

However, if you work for the subsidiary of an American multi-national, *never* refuse a posting to the States. It means that you are being groomed for future stardom and are virtually certain to be promoted. In a year or two you will return in triumph to a bigger job in your former company (with luck you could even become the MD). And there is no telling what 'goodies' the future may hold in store. Once you have been brainwashed the sky is the limit.

COMMITTEES AND WORKING PARTIES

One of the penalties of being a senior manager is that so much of your life is spent at meetings, listening to other people making fools of themselves. Meetings, by definition, are headless monsters, incapable of speedy decision-making, and are generally run by executives who are seeking to escape the perils of personal responsibility. 'United we stand, united we fall' is a comforting slogan for the professional ditherer. It means that his or her tracks will always be covered should the chickens one day come home to roost.

Be that as it may, you should always remain on your guard at meetings lest attempts be made to pass you the buck. Very often, following an inconclusive discussion, the suggestion will be made for a 'working party' to examine the facts and submit a report. Generally only a minority of those present will be required to serve on such a committee, thus isolating those who will 'carry the can'. If anything goes wrong it is they who will be blamed: if successful the credit will go to the chairman (of the original meeting, *not* the working party).

Never volunteer for working parties and vigorously resist any attempts to recruit you. Not only is the work invariably tedious, the time involved can be absolutely ruinous and can easily affect your job performance. Far from covering yourself in glory, you may well end up a nervous wreck through trying to do two jobs at once. Let those who have the time carry the banner. An ambitious executive sticks to what he or she does best.

PERSONAL ASSISTANTS

Many executives concentrate upon building up their empires, encouraged by job evaluation schemes that award points according to the number of people controlled. This can often be a somewhat short-sighted strategy since it makes them highly vulnerable to those periodic cost-cutting drives when every function is put on trial for its life. After all what a company gives it can also take away. It will not hesitate to do so when its survival is at stake.

However, since most executives work on the principle that the bigger the army the more senior its commander, an offer of more staff can be extremely tempting – the kind of opportunity that seems too good to refuse. And when such an offer is *personalised* ('It's high time we gave you a Personal Assistant') few can resist drinking from what may sometimes be a poisoned chalice. If your PA is a person who is well known to you then probably you have little to fear. But if he or she is a stranger recommended by someone else, watch out – you could be harbouring a cuckoo in your nest.

By the very nature of their jobs, PAs are both assistants and confidants: it is virtually impossible to keep secrets from them. If they are to carry out their duties as personal ambassadors, they need to know their bosses' innermost thoughts so that they can effectively communicate the various strategies. And even if they are assigned a less exalted role as paper-shufflers and glorified messengers, they are bound to have access to confidential information. Can you *really* trust such a person to keep his or her mouth shut? If not, the results could be pretty devastating.

Never take on a Personal Assistant until you have carried out a thorough background check and an equally searching interview. If you have the slightest doubts about the candidate's maturity or discretion, take no chances – reject at once. It is better to soldier on as you are than to run the risk of having your confidences betrayed. And beware of the PA who may be a 'double agent', having formerly worked for one of your rivals. It could well be that he or she has

71

been deliberately 'planted'. That seeming thoroughbred could be a Trojan Horse.

ADVISORY POSTS

For a staff employee to be offered a job in line management is a clear indication that the chosen individual is on the way up and is destined for bigger and better things. But offering the job of 'advisor' to a line manager is similar to taking a vote of 'no confidence' in a government and augurs badly for future prospects. Make no mistake: the nearer you are to the 'sharp end' of business, the better your chances of reaching the top. If you only provide a back-up service the road winds uphill all the way.

However, it is possible for you to be doing a good job in line management and yet still to be offered a move to 'staff'. Many ingenious explanations will be advanced ('We must have *well-rounded* people at the top'), but the more they try to 'sell' you the more you should beware: there may be a whiff of gunpowder in the air. Either somebody 'upstairs' has taken a dislike to you or, likelier still, such a person is trying to ease you out. Realising the importance of your current job, he or she may be keen to replace you with a more compliant individual.

Provided that you are a first-class performer you can nearly always fight off such plots – using the threat of resignation as your ultimate weapon. Good line managers do not grow on trees and your departure might cause a most embarrassing vacuum that would be quickly reflected in the 'bottom line'. The subsequent inquest would soon reveal why the company had lost such a valuable servant and heads more expensive than yours could roll. So stick to your guns and call their bluff. You are unlikely to be troubled again.

Being able to recognise a spurious offer is as important as snapping up genuine opportunities: all that glisters is not gold. Behind those honeyed words could lurk a ruthless will that sees you as an obstacle to some grand design, an expendable pawn in an executive power game. You will win far more respect by saying 'no' boldly than by appearing unduly anxious to please. Never depend upon someone else's judgement. The important issues you must decide for yourself.

CHAPTER ELEVEN

HOW TO CONQUER EXECUTIVE STRESS

– RULE –

Don't complain about stress, welcome it – what else weeds out the competition so well?

D o you suffer from recurring homicidal fantasies involving your boss? Do your colleagues strike you as insufferable bores? Do you daydream continually about beaches in Barbados? Are customers just a bunch of intolerant Yahoos? Answer but one of these questions positively and there is no doubt about it. You are deep in the throes of executive stress.

But take heart: all is not lost. There is light at the end of that windswept tunnel. What you must realise is that you are being tested – tested by the gods for an even bigger job and for a car which will be envied both by your enemies and your friends. You cannot expect life to be one long business lunch. Occasionally you must be prepared to pay the bill yourself.

Nevertheless, if you are going to survive this ordeal by neurosis, you had better start taking some countermeasures. Just as everything that glisters is not gold, so there are many pitfalls for the misguided enthusiast. While some activities are healthy and invigorating, there are others that can be psychologically lethal. Tread warily or you may find yourself trapped. Better tranquillisers than a padded cell.

GAMES

More executives have dropped dead while playing squash than during a major recession. Known to heart specialists as Stockbroker's Folly, it is a vicious, highly demanding game that can be relied upon to generate vacancies. By all means recommend it to your boss but resist the temptation to play yourself. As a person of ambition you cannot afford the carefree nonchalance of a sports-mad teenager. Conserve your energies for more worthy causes. You will find risks a-plenty in just doing your job.

For men, cricket is OK because it is so restful; indeed many a knotty problem has been resolved at long leg. Golf, however, should be played in moderation since it has a disturbing tendency to become over-competitive and you are unlikely ever to be fully relaxed. There is no point in exchanging the pressures of the rat race for the spurious bonhomie of the 19th hole. And few games seem to breed so many bad losers. The atmosphere in the clubhouse can be as sour as the office.

As far as more cerebral pastimes are concerned, the game to go for is unquestionably chess. Not only does it sharpen your conceptual skills, it also provides useful practice in intrigue and manoeuvre. There is something supremely satisfying in checkmating your opponent and watching his or her king go down to defeat: only a boardroom triumph has the same effect. And it is never too early to refine such skills. You could have need of them sooner than you think.

ILLICIT SEX

Some jaded male executives seek refuge in sex – often the expensive kind that comes gowned by Dior. Seeking to recapture the vigour of their youth, these venerable hell-raisers cut a pathetic figure. In smoky bars and frenetic discos they are the odd men out who believe they are 'in'. They have already lost what they most fear to lose: the capacity to enjoy themselves like carefree children.

All too often their mistresses are hardheaded ladies who refuse to be fobbed off with anything but the best. To them love is a commodity that has a price and that price is one which the market must bear. The fact that their tastes often bankrupt their lovers rarely causes them sleepless nights. Theirs is to spend, not to keep the score. Those are problems for bank managers and penny-pinching accountants.

The more cost-conscious Don Juans get involved with their secretaries, but these are notoriously ill-starred affairs. After the first few torrid encounters behind locked doors, the springs of romance quickly run dry and give way to the bedrock of fatigue and boredom. Apart from the ever present risk of the wife finding out, there are other trials that must be endured: the sly innuendo and the *double entendre*, the joshing nudge and the meaningful wink. The 'guilty' executive becomes a tragicomic figure, a deodorised Romeo with a paunch like Falstaff. No matter how hard he tries to retain his dignity, he is doomed to be stigmatised as 'a dirty old man'.

HOLIDAYS

The name of the game is relaxation: get as far away as possible from your normal routines. If you spend your life commuting in human cattle-trucks, fill your lungs with the air of moor and dale and drown your worries in pewter tankards. Rub shoulders with people who are content with their lives and who give not a fig for business values. Avoid men in sports jackets or stunningly well-groomed ladies. They are virtually certain to be fellow executive refugees.

Shed your city lifestyle like a snake sheds its skin and re-charge your mental batteries with new experiences. Don't ride if you can walk, don't walk if you can lie and use your radio just for listening to the weather forecast. Ignore fluctuating share prices, falling pounds and whatever it may have been that has 'shocked' the City. You can rest assured that Mammon will survive. Your holiday is too important to squander on such trifles.

Eat well but simply. You can do without coq au vin for a couple of weeks nor will your brain cease to function from lack of whisky or martinis. Think of yourself as a terrorist on the run from the police who risks being recognised if he or she enters a supermarket. Such harmless fantasies will do wonders for your waistline and will cause roses to replace the pallor in your cheeks. You may even begin to feel more romantically inclined and surprise your partner with an unexpected compliment.

Read widely on any subject (except making money) and let your

75

imagination run riot in unfamiliar terrain. Sail with Columbus to America or plant your standard at the summit of Everest. Outwit the KGB, baffle the Sûreté and respond to appeals for help from the Special Branch. It may be true that you have only one life but you can live many more in the theatre of your mind. All it takes is a little creativity. You will return to your desk like a rampaging lion, not the mournful bloodhound that you used to be.

CHILDREN – AND PARTNERS

Enjoy your children: they should be the light of your life and the hope of your future. Do not regard them as mere career distractions who should have the decency to keep out of your way. They are flesh of your flesh, not illegal immigrants. You have as much to learn from them as they have from you.

A child's world is coloured by curiosity; an adolescent's by doubts masquerading as certainties. Perhaps your own curiosity has been blunted by business, by long years of toeing the company line? If so, then here is your chance to start thinking afresh and to taste the delights of exotic new fruits. If your life has become a cultural desert, seek out cool oases that will refresh your spirit. Browse among bookshops, muse over music, and chance your brush on a canvas or two. Avoid anything that is even remotely competitive. Not everything can be measured in money.

Similarly, get involved in your teenager's social concerns and be prepared to put your principles on the line. It is not enough to murmur that he or she will 'see things differently' when they have had the 'rough edges' knocked off their idealism. It may be that *you* have thrown in the towel too early and have cocooned yourself with material possessions to quieten the prickings of your own social conscience? Stop thinking exclusively like a company man or woman and become a paid-up member of the human race. The trouble with renting yourself to a corporation is that you never get a rebate for lost opportunities.

If you are a male, remember that your wife, too, deserves her place in the sun. She has stood by you while you were clawing your way up and would do so again if you were on your way out. Even though the children may now have grown up, the balance of sacrifice is still in her favour (when did *she* last take a business trip or eat a five-star meal at company expense?). Get to know her more fully as a person, share her interests and encourage her to develop her own special talents. She will still be with you when the company is just a memory. And what she has to offer is far more enduring.

FRIENDS

Some people use material possessions to establish their place in the social pecking order. Nowhere is this trait more evident than among the executive classes with their cravings for swimming pools, luxurious cars and split-level houses with a 'minstrel's gallery'. Such a gargantuan appetite for material things is bound to cause stress, for as old wants are satisfied new ones spring up. It is like trying to climb a greasy pole: the greater your efforts the more frustrated you get.

Unhappily, most managers mix socially with other pole climbers, thus denying themselves the chance to get their lives into balance. At dinner parties, tennis clubs and even in the local pub, they seek out birds of their own grey feather and spend most of their time bewailing the iniquities of taxation and exchanging reminiscences of holidays abroad. Their conversations are peppered with references to country cottages, weekend sailing and cut-price wine offers in the Sunday press. State education is another obsession. There seems little that *any* government can ever do right.

To join in such materialistic rituals is simply to create a rod for your own troubled psyche: you will end up by believing that happiness is just a bigger deep-freeze. Just as giving up smoking requires an effort of will power, so steel yourself to avoiding these 'affluence freaks' and widen your circle to include some non-believers. Try to get closer to people who do their jobs not for the money but from a sense of service and who get their main satisfactions from helping others. The fact that they can be happy without being overrun by gadgets may strike you at first as being distinctly quaint, but as time goes on you will begin to sense their secret. It is not what they own but what they share willingly with others that enables them to be at peace with themselves.

77

Friends ought to be a good deal more than mere social wallpaper. They should enrich your life just as you should theirs. If their only contribution is to excite your envy, then they are running a race in which you should refuse to compete. Don't stay aboard a bandwagon that you cannot control. If you can't beat 'em, don't join 'em. Just jump off.

A PERSONAL PHILOSOPHY

Had you not been taking your work a shade too seriously you wouldn't be suffering from executive stress. This does *not* mean that you should become an apathetic drone doing as little work as possible for the maximum return (though, heaven knows, you would find yourself in some pretty august company). You simply need a *sense of proportion*. The world will not totter if you *pace yourself*.

Think. Would your firm close down if you were killed in a car crash? Would your partner leave you if you missed a promotion? Would your children despise you if you were unable to afford their school fees? Would your friends desert you for not buying a new car? Since all of these things are, hopefully, too absurd even to contemplate, it follows that to worry about them is merely self-defeating. People either like you or tolerate you for being what you *are*. There is no need to burden yourself with self-inflicted wounds.

Make no mistake: you need a religion. If you can believe in a god so much the better, but anything that cools your materialistic fever will do – it could be a course in yoga or doing voluntary work for a charity. By engaging in some activity that takes you out of yourself and replaces self-interest with a concern for others it is likely that your world will imperceptibly grow bigger and matters that once seemed important will now appear trivial (or at least less earth-shaking than you formerly believed). Not surprisingly, you will find that your performance at work will improve. Since you will no longer be tempted to labour over molehills you will have energy to spare for some real mountain climbing. Don't worry about the foothills if you are aiming at Everest. Make sure that the prize is worth the perspiration.

One final point. There is no particular virtue in working hard: what matters is whether you work *effectively*. If you persist in acting as though you were the centre of the universe, you will deny yourself the opportunity of ever finding fulfilment. So why not try to be a little less frenetic and suffer other fools as gladly as they suffer you? After all, you have nothing to lose except your nervous breakdown.

PART TWO

ELEVEN RULES FOR EXECUTIVE SUCCESS

CHAPTER TWELVE

HOW TO PICK A WINNING LEADERSHIP STYLE

– RULE –

Lead from the front – it's the only place to be if you want to make it to the top.

In management, as in life, you can be anything you want to be, provided that you want it badly enough and have the courage to persevere. And since as a manager you are expected to be successful, you have a clear vested interest in getting the best out of your people for it is *their* performance and results which determine *your* success. After all, if you could do everything single-handed then you wouldn't need subordinates, you could play every role yourself. But since such one-man shows are extremely rare in business, you had better learn quickly the arts of stage management – for if the play should fold you could be out of a job.

Being a good stage manager means being a good leader, knowing how to marshal your actors into a winning team. Rest assured that sooner or later each member of the cast is going to present you with problems and that many of your surprises will be anything but pleasant. Nevertheless, despite the vagaries of individual behaviour, it is you, the boss, who carries the heaviest burden since *you* create the ambience in which others must labour. It is your strengths (and your weaknesses) as a manager of people that can make all the difference between success or failure. There are six basic styles open to you.

TYRANTS

Although dinosaurs became extinct many millions of years ago, their human counterparts continue to flourish in the more primitive recesses of the executive jungle. Often to be found in the kind of family-owned concern where the founder is suffering from delusions of omnipotence, they are also common in American companies, notably at vice-presidential level. All types of dinosaur, large and small, have one fatal flaw that bodes ill for their companies: a total inability to adapt to change. As they blunder ponderously from one crisis to the next, they pose an increasing threat to the survival of the business.

The trouble is that you can't teach old dinosaurs new tricks – they are as inherently untrainable as man-eating sharks. And man-eaters they certainly are for what talented executives will put up with their tantrums? And when as a result of their autocratic posturings good people leave and are replaced by sycophants, then it is only a matter of time before the chickens of disaster come home to roost. At least half of all business catastrophes, whether of giant corporations or of more modest concerns, can be traced to the failings of these self-deluding tyrants – people who are accustomed to being treated like gods and for whom power becomes an hallucinatory drug, masking the reality of their human vulnerability.

Nevertheless, in companies that are ruled by such warped individuals one would expect to find smaller as well as bigger fleas, each capable of inflicting discomfort and irritation. There really is no excuse in modern business for firms which allow such bacilli to proliferate: they are a certain recipe for low morale and for every possible variant of human cussedness. Think carefully before you promote such people whatever their degree of technical competence. Executive leopards do not change their spots when they are permitted to climb the management tree. It simply gives them a vantage point from which to observe the approach of their prey.

SOFTIES

But while managerial tyrants are on their way out, there are still plenty of weak-kneed characters around whose long-term influence can be equally disastrous. These are the Softies, persons of excellent intentions but little business sense who tend to be over-protective towards their subordinates and to shield them from the consequences of their own mistakes. No wonder that they are so frequently over-worked; they spend most of their time solving other people's problems.

It is of course part of every manager's job to help subordinates develop their capabilities but this does *not* mean wet-nursing them *ad infinitum*. Softies, however, are like over-indulgent mothers who insist upon treating their teenage sons as though they were still helpless infants. Instead of encouraging their people to fight their own battles and to accept the inevitability of the occasional bloody nose, they allow them to run for cover at the first whiff of grapeshot and willingly retrieve any ground which has been lost. The result is that their subordinates never 'grow up' and become virtually incapable of taking tough decisions. This is why so many managers become lifelong procrastinators and have a deep-seated horror of 'committing' themselves. Soldiers who have never had to fire a shot in anger can hardly be expected to perform like veterans.

Softies are well-meaning do-gooders who would rather run a happy than an efficient ship. Far from developing people for greater responsibility, they gradually transform them into managerial eunuchs, bereft of initiative and moral courage. They have yet to learn that every fledgling must one day leave the nest and fend for itself in its natural environment. The fact that some will not survive is no great catastrophe. It is simply nature's way of preserving the species.

EXILES

These managers are virtually hermits, loners with an aversion to human relationships. They are the kind of people whose doors are never open and who are always too busy to see their subordinates – except to chastise them when they have committed some error. It is then that they display a penchant for that waspish turn of phrase that is sometimes favoured by dramatic critics, especially by those whose own plays have failed. Not that they are in any way frustrated intellectuals. They are just bullies who enjoy beating those weaker than themselves.

85

There is a glacial aura surrounding Exiles which even the most thick-skinned extroverts find intimidating. Far from treating subordinates as a precious resource to be helped and nurtured towards managerial manhood, they appear to regard them as troublesome wayfarers who have deliberately trespassed upon private land. 'You do your job and I'll do mine' is a characteristic response to appeals for help. They are like shepherds who cannot stand the sight of sheep, psychiatrists who are bored by the neuroses of their patients.

And so they live alone on their desert islands, feeling no need for the company of any Man or Girl Friday. When forced to communicate, they invariably do so in writing for they are great generators of forms and unreadable memoranda. Their desks, with their swelling mounds of neatly stacked paperwork, are like barricades constructed to ward off intruders and to impress upon them the need to 'get on or get out'. Here you will find no invitation to a friendly chat, nor will you be offered a morale-raising coffee. You will be made to feel that you have outstayed your welcome the moment you have received an answer to your question.

In short, here are managers who would have been happier as hermits or maybe as bird-watchers on the Upper Amazon. Why they were ever promoted remains a mystery. Perhaps their previous superiors grew tired of their silences and felt an overwhelming need just to *talk* to somebody? It would not be the first time that an individual has been promoted because of – not in spite of – his or her foibles.

OSTRICHES

These are managers who do not want to hear bad news: they would far rather believe that 'everything is OK'. Just as some Roman emperors would react to bad tidings by ordering the execution of the messenger who brought them, so Ostriches can turn exceedingly unpleasant when their placid lives are disturbed by a crisis. Immediately they set in motion ruthless witch hunts in order to flush out a few luckless scapegoats upon whom they can vent their outraged spleen. They have no tolerance whatever for human fallibility. Those who disturb their rest must by made to pay.

Not surprisingly, subordinates often go to great lengths to prevent them from withdrawing their heads from the sand. All communications are carefully doctored to eliminate even the suggestion of an emerging problem and any current skeletons are kept locked in their cupboards. Ironically, while Ostriches preen themselves upon their managerial efficiency, insulated from reality by their too loyal subordinates, it never seems to occur to them how fortunate they are to command people whose mission is to save them from themselves. These self-centred egotists are not merely devoid of gratitude, it is doubtful whether they are aware that such an emotion exists.

Nevertheless, their luck seems to know no bounds and they are frequently promoted far beyond their capabilities. It is they who get the credit for the work done by others, they who accept the plaudits for victories that others have won. Steadily they climb the executive ladder, leaving behind them a waste-land of frustrated ambitions and not a few poor work-horses who are completely burnt out. Such is the price which some companies pay for rewarding 'results' *without enquiring more closely into how they were achieved*. There is only one way of stopping the inveterate credit snatcher: demand evidence of his or her *personal* contribution.

RIP VAN WINKLES

While some managers give the appearance of being conscious, in fact they have been mentally asleep for years. These are the Rip Van Winkles, dreamy-eyed worshippers at the shrine of Morpheus, whose zest for creativity has long been buried through over-exposure to routine jobs. It is amazing how some companies expect employees to 'work their passage' by slaving away for years in managerial salt-mines in preparation for their anointment as 'effective executives'. While no one can become an Olympic hurdler without years of training and sustained self-discipline, neither is it necessary to spend very much time jumping over fences that are only one foot high.

Rip Van Winkles are managers who barely cleared such fences and thereafter lost all interest in the race. Nevertheless, as the years rolled by, they found themselves promoted into bigger jobs and surrounded by people to whom they could 'delegate' their work. Being basically uninterested in further progression, they then happily settled down in their feather-bedded ruts, doing what they were told to do but precious little else. Predictably enough, they are the least exacting taskmasters. All they ask is to be left alone.

Such zombies are often described as the salt of the earth – 'but if the salt hath lost its savour, wherewith shall it be salted?'. It is far more likely that they will infect their subordinates with their own acceptance of sloppy standards of performance and their characteristic aversion to new ideas. Indeed, it takes more than just a pinch of moral fibre to withstand the atmosphere created by such persons whose real interests, if any, lie outside their jobs. This is why so many able individuals pull up stumps and leave. They become tired of umpires who are always falling asleep.

DYNAMOS

The typical Hollywood portrait of big-company executives is one of all-action decision makers who live only for their work, dollar-crazed dervishes who lust after success. (British executives are a shade more dignified: they are also expected to read *The Times* and to comprehend menus written in French.)

However, regardless of nationality, all executives are required to take action and, more important still, to be *seen* to be doing so. A manager whose telephone never rings and who no one consults is a living affront to those dynamic business gods who expect their mortal followers to be eternally busy, enriching the shareholders if not themselves. Far from leading a sedentary life, ambitious executives must be superbly fit, scurrying endlessly from meeting to meeting and shrugging off boredom with iron self-control. There are few greater sins than to appear too philosophical, especially in the midst of a company-wide 'panic'. If everyone around you is losing their heads, then show some concern or you may lose yours too.

But if you want to be a Dynamo, make sure that your actions are really purposeful; you are not paid just to whistle hopefully in the dark. Get to the root of the problem as quickly as possible and move swiftly and decisively to bring it under control. Above all, contrary to the advice of those academic theorists who would have you wait until you have unearthed all 'the facts', do the best you can with the available information – if you linger too long the battle may be lost. Admittedly the dividing line between success and failure is often finely drawn and you must accept that there will be times when nothing will go right. But this does not mean that you can afford the luxury of waiting. You are expected to try to put out the flames yourself.

Finally, remember that whatever 'management style' you decide to practise will be critically appraised by your immediate subordinates. No matter how hard you work at being a good 'people person', it is your foibles, not your strengths, which will be most frequently discussed. The most that any boss can hope for is to be seen as only moderately incompetent, i.e. a damn sight less stupid than most of his or her peers. But surely you didn't expect to be successful *and* popular? People who live in jungles shouldn't complain about the heat.

CHAPTER THIRTEEN

HOW TO GET THE BEST FROM YOUR PEOPLE

– RULE –

Find out what motivates each individual – even dreams and fantasies can work in your favour.

E ven the most successful managers occasionally make mistakes and the bigger the mistake the more serious the consequences. Yet in many companies far more attention is lavished upon technical and commercial errors than upon those infinitely more widespread and damaging idiocies that lower morale and breed discontent. Let a key account be lost and all hell will break loose with much agonizing and soul-searching in the upper echelons. But let a key manager resign and he or she will merely be replaced. There is usually no witch hunt – just an embarrassed silence.

While some people leave to better themselves, many more depart because they feel unappreciated and despair of improving their relationship with their boss. Frequently it is not a question of some howling injustice, more a general feeling that 'my boss doesn't understand me'. And all too often such feelings are valid: the boss has indeed failed to find out what makes the person tick. Worse still, he or she may be using the wrong sort of 'motivator' – one which the subordinate finds utterly meaningless.

Now there are all kinds of motivators for all kinds of people: you must select the right carrots for particular individuals. This means getting to know them even better than they know themselves – which is by no means as daunting as it may sound. After all, it is always easier to diagnose others' strengths and weaknesses than to be objective about one's own. Psychiatrists never dream of trying to analyse themselves. It takes a perceptive *observer* to sift fact from fantasy.

MONEY

Despite the chidings of some behavioural scientists, for whom all monetary incentives would appear to be ignoble (a belief not reflected in the size of their fees), money remains for most executives an important inducement to extra effort. This is not because managers are excessively greedy – by comparison with some trade unionists they are ascetic monks. The importance of money is that it signifies *recognition* – of both individual contribution and personal achievement.

Or does it? Surely one of the most debilitating trends in modern industry has been the insidious growth of 'salary administration' with its accompanying edifice of bureaucratic procedures which have eroded the differentials between the excellent and the average? If the high flyer is rewarded with only a few crumbs more than the person who turns in a moderate performance, then what price money as an executive motivator? It is not that it has lost its inherent strength. Like a chained-up tiger it cannot break free.

Another factor that has emasculated the power of money – again, aided and abetted by the personnel bureaucrats – is the idea that everyone is entitled to an increase unless his performance has been positively disastrous (though in practice even this is sometimes glossed over). The result is that the money available for salary increases is allocated according to egalitarian principles instead of being used to recognise excellence. Such spurious 'fairness' can have only one end. Good people leave and mediocrities thrive.

Never be afraid to deny a salary increase to an individual who consistently fails to 'measure up' – and never be miserly with someone who is an outstanding performer. To be effective as a motivator money needs to be used *dramatically*, not doled out grudgingly in miserly amounts.

FEAR

Certainly you can, if you choose, intimidate your subordinates and run your department like a labour camp. But fear is generally a self-defeating motivator since it tends to produce new stresses and tensions which make improved performance extremely unlikely. Most sub-standard performers lack confidence in themselves and are hardly likely to be helped by a reign of terror. This does not mean that you should ignore their transgressions. You must learn to handle them in a *constructive* way.

Of course fear can be a two-edged sword. If everyone's hand is turned against you, you may become enmeshed in a guerilla war and have the greatest difficulty in achieving your objectives. For there are all kinds of acts of petty sabotage that mutinous subordinates can use to undermine you. And if you cannot rely upon the people you command then unquestionably you will be fighting a losing battle.

Consider, too, the effect upon yourself, particularly upon your peace of mind. Like some renaissance ruler surrounded by intriguers, relaxation will be a luxury that you cannot afford; even a friendly gesture could conceal latent treachery. Nor is there much point in having your subordinates obey you if they are far too apathetic to use their initiative. You will be little more than a chain-gang overseer in charge of people without interest or hope. And every one of them could be a potential assassin.

But as with every rule there is always the exception – in this case the gifted but indolent person who needs 'a shot in the arm' to re-awaken zeal. Such people will often respond to a little judicious needling aimed at encouraging them to pull their weight, especially if they are delegated challenging tasks. Once their vanity has been dented by a few home truths they are seized with a desire to prove themselves. Which simply goes to show that you cannot *always* be compassionate. Sometimes you have to be cruel to be kind.

PRAISE

Praise from the boss is, and always will be, one of the most powerful motivators to continued good performance. Apart from promotion or a thumping good salary increase, there is nothing to equal that warm inner glow when one's efforts are appreciated by those in high places. It is rather like winning a TV talent contest. Whereas before you were merely just another competitor, now you are bathed in the spotlight's glare, acknowledging the plaudits of an admiring audience.

All this, of course, is blindingly obvious; most of us have known it since we were first patted on the head. In recent years, however, praise has been 'discovered' by the behavioural scientists and re-cycled into something called 'positive reinforcement'. This, we are told, is the ultimate elixir, the motivator of motivators that will cure all ills. Never criticise subordinates, we are warned by these gurus. Keep on praising them and – presto! – all will be well.

Now, as every chairman knows, you can always rely upon 'man-agement experts' to overstate a good case to the point of absurdity and to obscure the simplest point in a welter of jargon: after all, it is through such tactics that they justify their fees. The current furore about 'positive reinforcement' is a perfect example of this ill-starred genre with its wild hyperbole and shameless huckstering. For while there are gullible managers there will be no shortage of panaceas. There is nothing easier to sell than hope.

By all means use praise, but use it *sparingly*, or it will quickly lose its motivational edge. If a person has done an outstanding job then tell him or her so *and do it quickly* – if you delay too long you will be wasting your time. But there is no need to operate like a beserk Father Christmas, showering praise upon all and sundry. Such egalitarian nonsense merely devalues the motivator. Your subordinates will conclude that you have gone soft in the head.

STATUS

Management is a competitive activity where individuals strive unceasingly to stand out from the crowd and to win for themselves some form of recognition. Frequently egged on by ambitious partners, some managers value the trappings of office almost as highly as their salaries and benefits. Indeed, given the choice between a modest salary increase and a more impressive-sounding job title, a surprising number would opt for the title. Human vanity knows no bounds. There is a touch of the peacock in all of us.

While such a craving for display may be considered somewhat childish, there is no point in burying our heads in the sand – managers are not motivated by reason alone. If a person's ego is massaged by the size of his or her office, or their spirits are uplifted by a few Lowry prints, then a wise boss will harness the power of these baubles to keep such people at peace with themselves. After all, what will motivate one person will have no effect upon another. As a boss your job is not so much to question a subordinate's values but to find the keys that will unlock good performance.

As many companies have found through bitter experience, the use of status symbols must be rigorously controlled; any private buccaneering must be fought tooth and nail. Indeed there is often more uproar over cars and carpets than even the quality of the food in the staff canteen. The golden rule, of course, is perfectly straightforward: managers of the same grade must be treated alike. And whatever is decided must be enshrined in company policy. Too much freedom in such matters can be fatal to morale.

Status symbols are prized not just for their intrinsic value but *for what they signify to other people*. They confirm an individual's place in the company hierarchy and perform the same function as badges of rank. When a manager is allotted his or her own parking space in the office car park, it is clear to everyone that here is someone to be reckoned with. And if such a person's new company car boasts an extra thousand c.c., the promotion announcement becomes a mere formality.

PARTICIPATION

If you persist in believing that you can do everything yourself then you are unlikely to survive to enjoy your pension: you are the managerial equivalent of a kamikaze pilot. Worse still, if you take all the decisions without consulting your subordinates you will find yourself skippering a most unhappy ship where open mutiny is a daily possibility. The days of the industrial slave trade are over. Not only is Jack as good as his master, Jill is more than a match for both.

Naturally, allowing your subordinates to participate in decision-making in no way reduces your personal accountability, it simply motivates them to do their best. And this, after all, is what leadership is about – not cracking whips like a galley-master but encouraging people to believe in themselves and to band together in a common cause. It is not enough to cry 'Follow me!' and to hurl yourself on to the enemy's guns. If the troops have decided that the attack is suicidal, you may easily find yourself charging alone.

Participation, then, is sheer common sense and will pay rich dividends if you use it wisely. It is *not* an excuse for 'passing the buck' nor need it result in 'consensus management' – so long as *your* finger remains on the trigger. Remember it is not 'enlightened' to behave like a private when everyone knows you have officer's rank. You will merely fall prey to those barrack-room lawyers who are only too eager to shoulder you aside.

So resist the blandishments of those 'behavioural experts' who would have you believe that authority is 'immoral'; *they* are not responsible for achieving results. In the competitive world of business enterprise, the race goes to those who react most swiftly – not to those who hide behind the smokescreens of committees. Use every ounce of knowledge that your people possess to get them committed to *your* decisions. But never forget that when things go wrong the buck will rightly stop with you.

TRUST

Kick a mule once and he may move a short distance. Persist in kicking him and he may not move at all. This is the snag with 'negative motivators' – the more they are used the weaker their effects. But if you can win the trust of those who work for you, a fire will be lit which they will tend for themselves. Instead of having constantly to push them, you can concentrate your energies upon planning for the future.

Trust, however, is a tender vine which withers easily if there is a sudden frost. It is no use demanding that people trust you; you must win your spurs by your deeds, not words. Any clumsy politicking, any double-dealing and your every action will be viewed with suspicion. You will simply be seen as an arch-manipulator for whom people are merely expendable pawns.

True, there may be those who will abuse your trust and these you should deal with swiftly and ruthlessly. Tiny minority though they may well be, they can quickly undermine the whole edifice of your authority, especially if they appear to be 'getting away with it'.

Expense-account fiddlers, three-hour lunchers – these are types you would do well to get rid of. There can be little sense of pride in a regiment where blatant malingering is gutlessly tolerated.

Trust means being able to turn your back without instantly having a knife buried in it. It means opening yourself up to public scrutiny and being strong enough to survive any painful home truths. Above all, it means *managing consistently* – for people will not trust those whom they cannot predict. 'Justice for all' is no idle phrase. There must be no blue-eyed boys or girls. Only fellow team members.

Of course, to be candid, you never really motivate anyone: you merely create the scenario wherein individuals motivate themselves. Far from being an executive Svengali, your every action consumed by self-interest, your role is that of a somewhat steelier Mr Chips, sparing the rod but never spoiling the child. It is only those who are lacking in sensitivity whose ideas on motivation are simplistically dogmatic. For there are no panaceas, no wonder drugs. *You simply learn from experience and use your best judgement.*

CHAPTER FOURTEEN

HOW TO BECOME A LIVING LEGEND

– RULE –

Project a strong image – the company grapevine will do the rest.

Every company has its quota of 'living legends', individuals whose deeds have made them virtually fireproof and who are regarded with awe by the lesser breeds. From London to Lagos, Bangkok to Bahrain, wherever folk gather around company camp fires, the latest exploits of these pin-striped immortals are lovingly recounted and eagerly dissected. Soon, as anecdote piles upon anecdote, it becomes clear that what is happening is a kind of ritual: the homage of 'losers' to absent 'winners'. So how can *you* carve a niche in this hall of fame? You must get yourself labelled in one of the following categories.

TURNAROUND EXPERTS

There is no surer way of entering the company pantheon than to demonstrate your prowess as a master mariner who can pilot a ship through the stormiest seas. The greater the losses and the more sluggish the cash flow, the more splendid your opportunity to become a Turnaround Expert and to bring your ship home safely into port. And if this means having to throw some ballast overboard, in the shape of the weaker members of the crew, why, then go ahead and do your duty. Those who survive will be doubly grateful that it was you who saved them from being eaten by sharks.

But top-class Turnaround Experts are no mere butchers. Suave and debonair, they are charm personified, perpetual smilers whose knives are well hidden behind an outward show of bonhomie. With their ready handshakes and toothpaste smiles, they are everyone's friend and beloved of all. But beware, behind that smokescreen of infinite chumminess lurk human tigers with one consuming obsession – to claw their way to the very top. And God help those who bar their path. Their careers will be snapped like broken twigs.

Still, if your appetite for power is sharp enough and you are unburdened by the prickings of a social conscience, then strive to become a Turnaround Expert for you will not be unwelcome in a host of companies. After all, once you have reached the topmost pinnacle there will be time enough to rejoin the human race and to demonstrate what a really nice person you are. And, amazingly, most of your sins will be forgotten. You will have only to cope with the occasional nightmare.

SOCIAL SUCCESSES

To be a resounding Social Success you do not need to be outstanding at your job but you must be prepared to work extremely hard. It will also help if you have an understanding partner with the temperament and virtues of a monk or nun. Indeed, unless you are ready to put your relationship at risk, you ought not to start something that your partner might finish. An occasional late night might be tolerated but not professional absenteeism.

Assuming, therefore, that you can placate your partner, then plunge headlong into those social activities which – like the 'bread and circuses' of ancient Rome – are believed by companies to purchase loyalty. Become the secretary of the Social Club. Organise visits to lowbrow shows. Mastermind the company sports day. Crown the winners of beauty contests. Act as MC at the Christmas Dance. Be present at all retirement presentations. But be sure to provide a *comprehensive* service. Be equally scrupulous in attending employees' funerals.

After a few years' hard slog, new and enticing vistas will begin to open up and you will find yourself moving in more elevated circles. Either you will become the company's official lobbyist (Executive in charge of Public Affairs) or you will be given the job of cosseting customers in five-star restaurants and exclusive clubs. And while you may not become an expert golfer or tennis player, you will be quite irresistible at the clubhouse bar with a fund of anecdotes for every occasion. In short, you will be a paid-up company mascot, a bon viveur with a job for life.

MISERS

Suppose as a father you refused to clothe your children except in rags, allowed your wife to buy only the plainest foods and declared that holidays were simply for spendthrifts who would never have a penny on a rainy day. The chances are that you would be regarded by your neighbours as a raving eccentric who was urgently in need of psychiatric treatment. Not so in business. There are many companies where meanness is a way of life, masquerading under the banner of 'financial prudence'.

If you happen to work for such a grasping concern, you have a first-class opportunity to make your mark and to amass those 'savings' which will lead straight to the boardroom. The key area for penny-pinching is, of course, salary increases – especially as applied to those older and less talented employees who would find it extremely difficult to obtain another job. 'Not good enough to promote but not bad enough to fire' – such employees are virtually imprisoned in their jobs and fall easy prey to the ruthless Miser. Fearful of putting their pensions at risk, they will usually endure even the most churlish treatment as they plod wearily towards the oasis of retirement. And while some swallow their pride and join white-collar unions, the majority cling to their hopes of better times and spend their weekends doing moonlighting jobs.

Misers, however, care not a fig for such problems. They are far too engrossed in building their reputations as hoarders of paper clips, flickers-off of switches and voracious vetters of expense accounts. Armed with the latest computer print-outs they rampage through their firms like demented axemen, lopping down the good trees as well as the diseased in their sycophantic zeal to please their superiors. And, sure enough, they win the prize that they are seeking: they become their companies' Financial Directors. Which simply goes to show that in some firms at least those who spread famine are the first to feast.

JOKERS

Business is full of po-faced robots for whom a slight dip in the sales graph is the end of the world. Totally devoid of outside interests, the only time they have a good laugh is when some major catastrophe befalls a competitor. Fingers flying over their beloved calculators (as they hasten to work out the potential benefits), it is only then that they may be observed to be smiling and, horror of horrors, *enjoying themselves*.

Strange then, that the amiable Joker, that rough-hewn begetter of a thousand belly-laughs, should be able to win a place in that executive Valhalla which is so often barred to more sober individuals. Invariably male, the Joker's secret is childishly simple: make 'em laugh but *never at each other*. In other words, it is always some *outside group* that bears the brunt of his wit, whether it be Women's Libbers, half-baked Lefties or ethnic minorities with language problems (deviant clerics are another favourite target). The effect upon his admiring listeners, in company canteens and sleazy bars, is to give them a feeling of effortless superiority over these luckless members of the human race who are apparently cursed with such comic defects. If you are a white male fascist and vigorously heterosexual, then clearly you are one of the *herrenvolk*: this is the essence of the Joker's message. It is one which, unhappily, still has some appeal to the more primitive denizens of the executive jungle.

And so the Joker becomes a recognised 'company character' who is regarded as possessing a heart of gold, though in fact he is a rather pathetic fellow who uses 'humour' to mask his lack of talent. In his element at trade association dinners ('Good old Tom!' cry his besotted cronies), he is a thoroughly unworthy company ambassador who can do serious damage to his company's image. For (think his critics) if this is the best his company can do, then perhaps we ought to look more carefully at their products and services? After all, a firm that sees fit to advance such a man may have plenty of skeletons in other cupboards.

STRAIGHT-SHOOTERS

Straight-Shooters are totally self-centred individuals, insensitive bullies with whiplash tongues. Priding themselves upon their no-nonsense directness, they behave towards their subordinates like hungry pikes who have succeeded in flushing out a shoal of minnows. The fact that they lose their most able people appears not to worry them in the slightest degree. They put it down to a lack of 'guts' and continue to snap at everything in sight.

Straight-Shooters abound in firms with elderly managements who are still fighting the battles of those far-off days when people could be treated as cannon-fodder. They talk constantly of 'cracking whips', 'kicking backsides', and 'sorting 'em out'– the vocabulary of the slave-gang overseer. It never occurs to them that by 'laying it on the line' they are advertising their lack of leadership, their gross insensitivity to other people's feelings. They are so obsessed with their 'tough guy' image that they would want to baton-charge a riot at a children's party.

Possessing all the subtlety of a bad-tempered rhino, S-S People are splendid recruiting agents for all those enemies of a free society who regard executives as mere white-collar thugs, the complaisant lackeys of greedy financiers. Those companies that encourage and promote such individuals are simply hastening the day of reckoning – not with 'the revolution' but with the bankruptcy courts. For where Straight-Shooters flourish there can be no flowering of initiative: persons such as these stamp out creativity and turn their companies into waterless deserts. The price of tolerating such boorish indi- viduals – worse still, of treating them as 'company immortals' – is the steady erosion of the company's future. Talent rarely prospers in a prison cell.

MAVERICKS

Some people are born to greatness; others thrust greatness upon themselves by making a religion of their individualism and steadfastly refusing to toe the line. Most Mavericks fall into two main categories: the harmless Peacock and the lethal Laser.

The Peacock is just a male show-off who uses his appearance to attract attention, a bumpkin Beau Brummel with few other talents. He is chiefly to be found in advertising agencies, though he sometimes turns up in industry in PR departments, those busy beehives of misguided enthusiasms. There is no great harm in the elegant Pea- cock; indeed, he brings a touch of colour into humdrum lives. It is only when he aspires to intellectual greatness that one's patience begins to fray at the edges. After all, there is nothing more ludicrous than a man who claims to be meditating when it is obvious that he is merely half asleep.

Lasers are altogether more formidable mavericks: they are vigorous crusaders against company cant. Highly argumentative and suspicious of authority, they can be relied upon to pierce through any policy announcement and to communicate its 'true' meaning to the mystified masses. With their cynical interpretations of top management changes and their eye for any shift in the balance of power, Lasers are rather like subversive shepherds who believe it their duty to lead their flocks astray.

Why, then, are they tolerated by those apostles of 'double-speak' who are so frequently found in the higher echelons? For two reasons. Firstly, they are usually quite outstanding at their jobs and are widely respected throughout their companies. Secondly, they often have powerful connections (in politics and the media) which, were they to be victimised, they would not hesitate to use. Few companies will risk a public relations disaster; it is far safer to ignore these irritating gadflies. For while sticks and stones may not break any boardroom bones, a publicity debacle is invariably painful – and high-priced heads are virtually certain to roll.

Becoming a Company Immortal is not, of course, the only way of ensuring your survival. If you are good at your job and have attended the right schools (fee-paying for oil companies, state for engineering), then you will probably coast gracefully towards your pension and the blessed relief of a country cottage. But if you feel the need for further insurance and are not afraid of the spotlight's glare, then join the ranks of these company immortals. You need only be able to live with yourself.

CHAPTER FIFTEEN

HOW TO MEET THE RIGHT KIND OF PEOPLE

– RULE –

Build your own private mafia – the most valuable pipelines are always underground.

S uccessful senior managers and prime ministers have at least one thing in common: both need to forge an effective foreign policy. Just as the politician must safeguard his or her country's interests abroad, so executives need to build up their external contacts, partly for business and professional reasons, partly as an insurance against possible future catastrophes. For in the volatile world of modern business no one is exempt from the law of the jungle. Many a seemingly impregnable executive has been ousted from the office in a matter of hours. The prudent manager, like the far-sighted statesman, hopes for peace but is prepared for war.

Establishing a network of useful contacts requires both steady application and entrepreneurial flair: you must remain constantly alert to exploit your opportunities. While there will be many occasions when you meet new people in the natural course of your business life, it is unwise to rely upon such chance encounters since many of them may be of only minor value. Instead, decide what kind of fish you want to catch and then frequent those waters where they are most likely to be found. Use the right sort of bait to attract their attention and strike swiftly and decisively when you get a bite.

PROFESSIONAL ASSOCIATIONS

Any executive worthy of his or her company car will keep in touch with the appropriate professional associations and attend their meetings from time to time. It is not just a question of keeping up to date, there are also opportunities to make valuable contacts. This is particularly the case when the visiting speaker is a 'celebrity' in his or her field and is therefore likely to attract a large audience. Lurking among all those dignified faces could be people with the power to influence your career.

It is no use remaining anonymous – you must deliberately draw attention to yourself. Asking questions is the most obvious ploy, but it is one that should be used with great discretion otherwise people will think you are a chronic exhibitionist. To generate goodwill when asking a question always take care to be scrupulously polite – indeed, preface your remarks with a touch of flattery. For while many experts are hopeless speakers, they will appreciate your efforts to shield them from the truth. And when you seek him or her out during the coffee interval, your invitation to lunch will be graciously accepted.

If your questions have sparked off a lively discussion, you may well be approached by other members of the audience who may wish to exchange ideas with you. Once again, here is a chance to make new friends whose help could one day prove extremely useful. Make sure that you exchange business cards with those whom you discover are particularly influential. While chief executives should be your primary target, some personnel managers can be a sound investment.

SPEAKING ENGAGEMENTS

Sometimes the boot may be on the other foot and you may be invited to give a talk yourself. However miniscule the fee that you may be offered, accept with the speed of a striking cobra; prestige cannot always be measured in money. As every ambitious manager knows, there are times when it is foolish to be over-acquisitive. The publicity value is a reward in itself and until you are well known you must be content with a pittance.

Whatever the occasion, great or small, never neglect to prepare yourself thoroughly: 'doing your homework' is the key to success. Nothing is more impressive to a management audience than a speaker who has devised a well-thought-out plan which he or she then executes with flair and panache. The greater your enthusiasm the greater your impact and the more likely you are to command respect. For despite the traditional reserve of business executives, there is nothing they like better than a flamboyant speaker, all fire and brimstone and apocalyptic fervour. After years of listening to droning bores they have often given up hope of being kept awake. To encounter a speaker who is knowledgeable *and* entertaining induces feelings of undying gratitude.

Having made a tremendous impression during your presentation, it is time for you to bring the temperature down in order to create the climate for a relaxed discussion. This means, above all, that you must demonstrate the ability to suffer fools gladly: sarcasm and irony should be strictly *verboten*. No matter how much you may be tempted to make mincemeat of a questioner who is clearly no more than a pompous buffoon, treat his or her remarks as though they actually made sense (any further tomfoolery will be dealt with by the group). A really confident speaker has a knack of releasing his audience's inhibitions – of motivating them to express their true concerns. In psychological terms this means descending from Olympus and joining in the discussion as one of the group.

Remember, you never know who may be in the audience and as you become more skilled your fame will spread. Soon the invitations will begin to roll in and you will find yourself billed at important conferences as 'an acknowledged authority' who is 'a lively speaker'. Naturally your prowess will become known in the company and in most cases approving heads will nod. You will be regarded as a first-class public ambassador who, despite his fame, remains loyal to the company. Of course such faith could be easily shattered should you receive the right offer from another firm. But in the meantime you can reap another useful benefit. You can be much more aggressive when negotiating your fees.

WRITING ARTICLES

Writing articles for business journals is a potent method of building a reputation and of publicising your talents to a wider audience. As a glance at many of these journals will confirm, you do not need to be a literary giant: the requirement is for practical, down-to-earth articles written in a clear and readable style. You ought not to be deterred from trying your hand by the myth that editors are sadistic ogres who delight in sending out rejection slips. Most are pragmatic, level-headed types who are only too pleased to receive freelance material, especially if it is based upon personal experience.

Naturally you must expect a few early setbacks, for writing, like any skill, demands constant practice. But sooner or later, if you persist at your task, your by-line will appear in all its glory and you will have taken your first step towards becoming a 'name'. Now is the time to prepare yourself for whatever reaction the next issue may bring – for your piece may spark off a lively correspondence. However, should a critical letter wound your pride, do not rush into battle like an angry boar. A mere academic quibble is hardly worth answering, but if the criticism is more solidly based an elegant riposte will do you no harm. It is all grist to the mill of your publicity campaign. Nevertheless, there are times when it is better to turn the other cheek. For example, should other protagonists enter the lists and begin to exchange insults and clumsy invective, resist the temptation to join in the fray. Instead, maintain a dignified silence and draft a reply for one of your friends to sign.

Like speaking engagements, articles in the journals can cause doors to open that would otherwise have remained firmly closed. Letters may arrive inviting you to speak at conferences or seeking your advice on some intractable problem. Not least, since your name will have been noted by headhunters, you could soon be receiving some attractive phone calls. All this could happen after a mere handful of articles. The pen can indeed be mightier than the sword.

CLUBS

There are three types of club where it is possible to make useful contacts: business, sporting and social/charitable. The most common example of a business club is the Chamber of Commerce but you ought not to expect too much from these worthy assemblies – many are dominated by small-town shopkeepers who spend most of their time complaining about income tax. A far better bet is your local branch of the Institute of Directors for here you will meet men and women who run their own businesses, as well as other executives like yourself who are eager to expand their circle of friends. Be warned, however, establishing such contacts does not come cheaply and you must be ready for some expensive encounters at the bar.

But if you have a sympathetic bank manager and an understanding spouse then by all means take the plunge – you do not even have to be a bona fide director!

Golf is the most favoured sport among budding male tycoons and in many large companies is *de rigueur* for anyone aspiring to a top-hat pension. Unfortunately, it is a game that reeks of competitiveness and can cause as many feuds as a promotion decision. It should only be played if you are prepared to lose gracefully (and often) to those whose favours you are seeking to enjoy. But if you are incapable of dissembling your feelings in defeat, then you would do better to take up a game like chess which has a calming effect upon even the most sensitive ego. Sailing is another relaxing pastime for both men and women and seems to inspire more smiles than scowls. It is also less expensive than golf – at least in the long run. For whereas many golfers are notorious whisky guzzlers, most male sailors are content with their manly pints (lady mariners usually take lime with their lagers).

Joining groups like the Rotarians or the Round Table is a splendid way of contributing to charitable causes and also of making new business contacts. There is traditionally an aura of good fellowship at their meetings which can easily spill over into other spheres and provide you with a network of well-informed agents. And there are many occasions in modern business when it can be invaluable to have accurate grass-roots intelligence about impending developments in your local community. Admittedly you may have to endure the occasional boring luncheon, but this is a small price to pay for the potential benefits – particularly the chance to build your own private mafia.

POLITICAL ACTIVITIES

While business people in general are often highly critical of politicians, perceptive executives need no reminding of the solid advantages of a political 'connection'. After all, an ambitious politician has much in common with a thrusting executive. Both are natural 'fixers' and 'horse traders', accustomed to keeping their ears to the ground. Both recognise the importance of 'knowing the right people' and of projecting themselves in the most favourable light.

Despite the impressive growth rates for left-wing millionaires, most executives regard right-wing parties as the natural custodians of business interests. This can be short-sighted. True, most would-be Bentley and Jaguar owners are likely to find fewer kindred spirits in the beery boisterousness of a working men's club, but the astute executive should always attempt both to run with the hare and to hunt with the hounds. In other words, it is foolish to allow your own personal predilections to govern your choice of political contacts. There are times when the friendship of one powerful trade unionist can be worth a whole regiment of right-wing MPs.

You do not need to be a political activist in order to get the best of both worlds. A quiet donation to an appropriate cause, a few words of sympathy 'off the record', the occasional letter seeking 'advice' – these are the ploys that a person of discretion uses to strengthen his or her political fences. There is no need whatever to become identified with any sectarian political objective, still less with the 'wild ones' of either party. By refusing to stray from the middle ground you will command the respect of those 'moderate elements' who know a fellow pragmatist when they see one. All successful politicians have learned how to face both ways. They will not think less of you if you do the same.

You may have to wait some time before your pragmatism pays off, but when it does so the results can be pleasing. For example, a major shift in company policy can be discreetly tested for 'political acceptability' before it is actually put into practice (a major advantage for a multinational company). Then again, news may reach you of proposed legislation that may enable your company to lay contingency plans. Not least, during one of your 'undercover' visits to the House, you could be 'tapped' for a job in the public sector – one which could lead to even bigger things. You are unlikely to be asked whether you are a party member. You will already have shown that you can play the game.

Building up your contacts is like taking out insurance: the worst may never happen but you are covered if it does. Not only will your value to your company increase, you will also be less vulnerable to those sudden shifts of fortune that can so easily disrupt the most promising career. It is no use bewailing your accursed luck should you one day find yourself out of a job, the victim of a shake-out following changes at the top. Though you may be hoping for sunshine, be prepared for rain. An umbrella of contacts is your best protection.

CHAPTER SIXTEEN

HOW TO BECOME FAMOUS OUTSIDE HEAD OFFICE

– RULE –

Show that you've done your homework – the tougher your questions the more they'll respect you.

If you happen to be a senior head office executive, then you cannot expect to be universally loved. Indeed for those who labour in the remoter vineyards – be they factories, offices or construction sites – you are little more than a sybaritic drone, a living affront to the business virtues. Such is the price of fame. Having soared like an eagle to the top of the tree, you are constantly being mistaken for a work-shy cuckoo.

Nevertheless, like any good commander, you must occasionally inspect your far-flung outposts in case those on watch are tempted to fall asleep. There is no substitute whatever for a personal visit: to rely upon reports is simply asking to be misled. As every experienced manager knows, what may appear from afar to be a tranquil oasis may turn out to be a veritable Sodom and Gomorrah. To assume that 'no news is good news' is to court disaster. You owe it to yourself to take a closer look.

But be warned – once it is known that you are coming a whole series of countermeasures will be triggered off. Offices will be tidied, gangways cleared and even the more youthful male managers will invest in a haircut. Relations between executives and their attractive secretaries will temporarily lose much of their customary bonhomie and there may be outbreaks of skirts where once jeans reigned supreme. Everyone will be at his or her best in an effort to convince you that all is well. And sooner or later as you make your rounds you are bound to encounter some of the following types.

STIRRERS

Here are people who have been positively longing for your visit: there are so many things that they feel you ought to know. Often individuals who have been passed over for promotion, they nurse their grievances like those tropical plants that need constant attention in order to survive. Rarely a day passes without their being lovingly watered and their histories recounted to anyone who will listen. It is not merely that they feel that they have had a 'raw deal'. They are convinced that they are the victims of vicious conspiracies.

Having little to lose they will not hesitate to 'name names', though they prefer to infiltrate rather than to attack head on. Far from designating their enemies as fools, they generally tend to damn them with the faintest of faint praise – to scatter innuendos instead of making accusations. They are masters of the pregnant pause and know how to engineer a suggestive silence. They would rather that you drew your own conclusions – as long as these are based on *their* version of the facts.

Stirrers are well aware of those unwritten codes that encourage mutual loyalty between boss and subordinate and will rarely be crass enough to infringe them directly. For example, after regaling you at length about a particular local problem and having given you their views on how it should be solved, they will frequently conclude by saying 'X doesn't agree with me – but I'm not at all clear what the difficulty is'. Thus, at a stroke, they portray their superiors as unfeeling Neros who continue to fiddle as the conflagration spreads – while they, the ever public-spirited Stirrers, are forced to stand by and watch the blaze.

Do not be taken in by these serpentine characters; they know no loyalty other than to themselves. In their attempts to undermine the boss's credibility, they are driven by ambition and a desire for revenge, not by any feelings of corporate loyalty. You have only to investigate one of their innuendos to uncover a whole snake-pit of half-truths and distortions, each cunningly designed to lead you astray. There is only one effective serum against these human vipers. Get them off the payroll as quickly as possible.

AXE GRINDERS

Like their more Machiavellian colleagues, the Stirrers, Axe Grinders also look forward to your visits since they see them as an opportunity to do some special pleading and to impress their opinions upon you personally. Essentially they are frustrated Edisons, perpetual generators of half-baked ideas which their local managements have turned down flat. Bloody but unbowed, they await your arrival like a prisoner in the death cell who is expecting a reprieve. Being totally impartial and intelligent to boot, you are (so they think) bound to support them.

Naturally, you disappoint them, being no more sympathetic than their own superiors. This is hardly surprising since any proposal put forward by a Grinder is virtually certain to be both technically unsound and catastrophically expensive. Axe Grinders, however, live in a fantasy world where shortage of funds is never a problem to dashing superpersons like themselves. The only demons who inhabit this Nirvana are those cloth-headed bosses who refuse to see sense.

However, it is no use merely swatting them like a troublesome mosquito for they mean no harm and seek only to do good. They genuinely have the company's interests at heart but have yet to learn how to present a case. Listen to their ideas and let them down gently by asking them questions about the 'how' and the 'why'. The sooner they learn to think through their ideas, the more quickly they will become effective contributors. Their problem is not that they lack ability but that their enthusiasm is greater than their common sense.

COVER-UP EXPERTS

Every organisation has its skeletons in the cupboard that it is anxious to conceal from the world at large. The same is true of every part of the company – there is sure to be some dust under almost any carpet no matter how impeccable its appearance may be. The point to remember when you are visiting an 'outpost' is that things are *never* as smooth as they seem. It is not that you will be told any downright lies. You will be shown the headlines but not the small print.

Occasionally, however, you will meet the Cover-Up Experts, people for whom your visit is a serious threat. Instantly recognisable by their effusive welcomes – a bone-cracking handshake is the male's speciality – they seek to convince you that they are good-natured 'straight-shooters' and to create an impression of dynamic efficiency.

Show but a flicker of interest in any aspect of their work and they will swamp you with statistics, confuse you with charts, and run rings around you with erudite ratios. In short they will try to 'blind you with science' in the hope of blunting your critical edge.

The only way of dealing with these tricksters is to slow them down and then move in quickly for the kill. Never allow them to get into their stride – keep on asking questions and challenging the answers. Gradually it will begin to dawn on them that they are facing a professional who has done his or her homework. It is then that you will start to penetrate their defences and find out what they have been trying to hide.

You need not only a sharp brain when dealing with this person: you must also be prepared to use your eyes. Watch for those moments when they glance away from you or squirm uneasily in their padded chairs. Look out for those drumming fingers, those imperceptible frowns and those offers of coffee following a crucial question. It is more than likely that you have begun to draw blood and that in boxing terms they are 'on the ropes'. Never hesitate to exploit your advantage. People such as these are not worth generous treatment. They have won too many bouts by using dubious methods.

APPLE POLISHERS

Have you ever had a dream in which you were a world-famous celebrity, the idol of duchesses and the friend of kings? If so, then here is your chance to make your dream come true if only for a few delicious hours – for there is no one more skilled than the Apple Polisher at manipulating your secret delusions of grandeur.

These human sheep in executives' clothing are dedicated to gratifying your every whim since they believe (not irrationally) that many top managers have an insatiable craving to have their egos bolstered. Knock on any door and they will open it for you. Ask and they will do their best to oblige. They are the sort of people who if it rained at a wedding would cheerfully steal the bride's umbrella for you.

They do, of course, present a searching test of your emotional maturity. If you enjoy them fawning around your feet and treating you as though you were a feudal lord then there is little hope that you will see through their wiles and perceive the self-interest that lies beneath. But you have only to watch how they behave with their subordinates to realise that you are not loved just for yourself. Should anything not be going according to plan, their honeyed accents turn into querulous barks. It is painfully clear that their courtesies are reserved for those with the 'muscle' to advance their careers.

There is no point in fencing with these india-rubber people: show them right away that flattery cuts no ice. Light your own cigarettes, open your own doors and insist upon lunching in the staff canteen. Give them no opportunity to lick your shoes and concentrate your efforts upon assessing their results. You will frequently find that all is not well and that there are many grave weaknesses which are easily uncovered. This is hardly surprising since hard work and energy are not virtues to which they attach much store. They have always found sycophancy far more rewarding than any amount of honest toil.

WORK-HORSES

Every company has its Work-horses – those faithful, indestructible, long-serving employees without whom the business could not survive. High Flyers may come and go, Boards may totter and be replaced but dear old Work-horses plod on forever, ploughing The Field of a Thousand Chores. Content to remain 'also rans', they have no yearning to win a major prize. They simply want to be left alone to graze in those pastures which they know so well.

This does not mean that you can afford to ignore them when, Zeus-like, you descend upon their plants or offices. Indeed, far from concentrating exclusively upon the whizz kids, go out of your way to express your appreciation of their unflagging devotion to the corporate weal. While you may not be able to offer them any tangible reward – they will almost certainly have reached their salary ceilings – a few kind words and a pat on the back will infuse new vigour into their tired old bones. After all, they have stood by the company through many a storm when more fainthearted crew members were abandoning ship. And even though the weather may now be calmer, who can be sure how long it will last?

115

Talk to the Work-horses, enquire about their families and listen carefully when they tell you about their problems at work. Having no axe to grind and being devoid of ambition, the chances are that they are speaking the truth – and impartial intelligence is hard to come by in business. Should they be critical of some aspect of the operation, you can be virtually certain that they are on the right track. Only a person who has opted out of the rat race can afford the luxury of being frank.

BOLSHIES

Occasionally – very occasionally – you will meet someone who is out for your blood. These are the Bolshies, dare-devil jugglers with their managerial careers whose waspish tongues have made them renowned and feared. It is not that they have anything against you personally. You merely represent the hated 'system' which they regard as unfair and intrinsically corrupt.

What are such individuals doing in business – ought they not to be employed as professional agitators or perhaps as Intourist guides in Moscow? Not at all. Basically they are disappointed promotion seekers, people who feel that they have been deliberately thwarted by persons of miniscule managerial talent who saw them as a threat and barred their progress. They believe themselves to be surrounded by rogues and mountebanks who have attained their positions by mindless subservience and who would be incapable of running that proverbial sweetshop. It never seems to occur to them that *they* may have their shortcomings too. They find it more comforting to feel conspired against by an internal mafia of highly paid clowns.

You need not shed any tears for Bolshies – their perpetual nit-picking would alienate a saint. They are masterly i-dotters and crossers of t's, unable to resist correcting you on the smallest detail and revelling in their mastery of technical trivia. Nor will they lose any opportunity of insinuating that they regard you as a member of the idle rich. 'Come to see how the other half lives?' is one of their favourite greetings as you enter their offices.

There are two ways of handling Bolshies: you can either ignore them or resolve to give as good as you get. Ignoring them is not a particularly effective ploy since it is merely likely to inflate their egos and to strengthen their delusions of intellectual superiority. Adopting a consistently aggressive posture is far more likely to bring them to heel. This demands that you are sure of your facts and have enough strength of character to ram your points home. But once you have survived this ordeal by combat you will find them treating you with a new respect. After all, it is no surprise to be bitten by an angry alsatian. To be savaged by a seemingly innocuous lapdog is not only startling but much more memorable.

The image that you should present when visiting a company outpost is one of friendly yet businesslike curiosity: you have come not to hinder but to help if you can. Counter any suspicions that you are an armchair theorist by 'taking your coat off' and making a positive contribution. The more you know about local problems – which means studying them carefully *before* your visit – the more respect your views will command. But if you arrive trailing clouds of self-satisfied ignorance, you will quickly be classified as a useless drone. And one day such a label could hurt you badly. Among those 'peasants' could lurk a future king or queen.

CHAPTER SEVENTEEN

HOW TO KEEP THE IDEAS COMING

– RULE –

Cultivate creative people – lack of ideas can be a terminal condition.

Attending the occasional conference or seminar can be a good thing. It can provide a respite from the daily pressures, give you a chance to make new contacts and even soften the memory of that missed promotion. Above all, for a few fleeting hours or days it can plunge you into a world of make-believe management where steely-eyed executives with laser-beam intellects peer courageously into an unknown future. It is a time for philosophising, a time for reflection, and a time to give thanks for your expense account.

Yet despite its potential for relaxed good fellowship, a conference is not something to be attended lightly, especially if you are hoping for some kind of pay-off – a new idea, perhaps, with which to dazzle your boss. Indeed, for every conference that proves a success there are at least four others that will waste your time and send you home thinking murderous thoughts about those whose pockets you have helped to line. By then, of course, it is far too late and no amount of complaining will bring back the fee. What you need to recognise *before* you enrol is that attending a conference is like a game of chance. The odds are stacked against you right from the start.

THE PILGRIMAGE

Virtually every aspect of management has its quota of cult figures: erudite economists, master marketeers, flamboyant financiers and, most suspect of all, over-confident oracles from the groves of academe. Some, like Cassandra, utter dire warnings; others bring tidings of wondrous new techniques. But of one thing at least you can be absolutely certain – they will always recommend that you buy their books.

Worshipping such idols is a harmless enough pastime, provided that you recognise that their feet are made of clay. However impeccable their credentials or impressive their experience, it is no use expecting them to solve *your* problem for they lack that most vital of ingredients: first-hand knowledge. The most you can expect is that they will spark off a thought which may enable you to deal with the problem yourself. And while this is by no means an inconsiderable benefit, it may not be the product that you were hoping to buy.

A professional, of course, will acknowledge his or her limitations: it is the charlatans and con-people who will promise you the earth. Some of the most dangerous of these predators lurk in the steamier swamplands of the 'behavioural sciences' where reason sits unbidden like a spectre at the feast. Leadership experts whom no sane person would follow, psychologists brandishing mind-bending tests, motivational miracle workers with infallible formulae – there is no shortage of clowns in this raucous circus. But since there will always be a market for managerial black magic, there is no reason to suppose that such people will ever starve. Most, in fact, do very well indeed for hope springs eternal in the hearts of the gullible.

THE FASHIONABLE TOPIC

In management, as in music, the tide of fashion ebbs and flows as new panaceas replace the old. For example, only a decade or so ago most male managers could scarcely face themselves in their shaving mirrors unless they had attended a seminar on management by objectives. Today it is the turn of 'time management', 'assertive management' and a dozen other brands of executive snake-oil, all of which are claimed to make a new person of you ('effective executive' is the term generally used).

Doubtless many of these nostrums work well enough, given the right combination of faith and persistence – and provided that the boss is reasonably supportive. But if a manager's creativity has been ridiculed into oblivion in a company where top management is half asleep, it is most unlikely that he or she will be 'born again'. After all, one cannot turn vinegar into sparkling champagne, nor expect a lame duck to display the courage of a lion. *Plus ça change, plus c'est la même chose* is the predictable epitaph of even the best of ideas in companies where inertia is a way of life.

Nevertheless, there is no harm in prowling these 'techniques bazaars' since you may be fortunate enough to pick up a bargain which, though unusable in your present company, could well come in handy should you decide to leave. For example, it would certainly help to give you an up-to-date image when you are swapping gins and tonics with selection consultants. Always on the look-out for an 'up-market' candidate, they tend to respect what they do not understand.

THE PROFESSIONAL GET-TOGETHER

The annual conference of your professional institution may not be as fun packed as a weekend in Las Vegas – but you should never miss it if you aim to keep in touch. The speakers may be boring, the food mediocre and the waiters as surly as harem eunuchs. No matter. You are not there to savour the *dolce vita*. You are there to enlarge your circle of contacts and to establish yourself as a person to be watched.

Behind those potted plants in the hotel lounge (still more in the chumminess of the 'American Bar') a whole new world of opportunity can unfold that is yours for the taking if you are sufficiently adroit. Decide in advance who you would like to meet and, if you lack a friend at court, then introduce yourself. If your quarry has given a paper or has written a useful article, you have a perfect opportunity to make your mark since few speakers or writers are immune to flattery. There can be few greater compliments than to be asked for one's opinion, however idiotic the question may be. At least it shows that *someone* cares – that all that solitary labouring has not been in vain.

There are many other exciting potential benefits from the Get-Together: hearing who is 'in' and who is 'out'; rumours of new contracts being put out to tender; mutterings of senior vacancies not yet advertised; leakages about a competitor's marketing plans. With your ear to the ground and your lips tightly sealed, you can recover your expenses in a matter of hours – a few rounds of drinks can reap a golden harvest. There is no need to waste money employing 'industrial spies' when confidences are being scattered like confetti at a wedding. The moving listener listens and, having listened, moves on. There will be time enough later for decoding the messages.

THE EXPERT FORECAST

It is surprising how much hard-headed managers are prepared to pay for a tantalising glimpse of what the future may hold. Like bird-watchers peering at some mist-enshrouded pool in the hope of spotting a rare species of duck, they reverently gather around the crystal ball in the hope of penetrating the future's secrets. The presiding experts are, of course, no fools and will always pitch their prophecies at least ten years hence. This at once marks them out as persons of distinction, seers who are impervious to management myopia. It also means that if their predictions fail, their audiences will have long since forgotten what they said.

Some of the perennial favourites at these fortune-telling sessions include: 'economic trends over the next ten years'; 'the microchip world of 2001'; and, most hilarious of all, 'motivating managers in the age of robotics'. With all of these topics we are invited to leave reality behind and to plunge headlong into a world of fantasy, peopled by superpersons and creative robots who can solve any problem at the flick of a switch. The question that is never answered by these over-confident star-gazers is what will happen to all our redundant workforces? Will they be permanently spaced out on hallucinatory drugs? Legally compelled to watch daytime TV? Or encouraged to emigrate to the Upper Amazon to build multi-purpose leisure centres for primitive tribesmen?

Who knows? Certainly not the experts – they are as likely to be wrong as any fortune-teller. And for the simplest of reasons: the future cannot be predicted, it can only be *made*. It is what we do *today* that makes our tomorrows, not casting our hard-earned cash down wishing wells.

GETTING AWAY FROM IT ALL

Executive responsibility is not *always* a stimulant since 'challenge', like beauty, is in the eye of the beholder. If you are bored with your job and your career is stagnating, an invitation to spend a day away from the office can be very attractive – especially if there is no admission charge and even the buffet lunch is free. This explains the continuing popularity of executive 'jamborees', those strange, cosmopolitan gatherings where everything is arranged for your comfort and pleasure. All you have to do is to relax and enjoy it for he or she who hath paid nothing hath nothing to lose.

Easily the most popular of these mid-week breaks is the training film preview, particularly when the films feature well-known comedians with the gift for making us laugh at ourselves. Though the laughter at times may be somewhat brittle, especially if the manager is accompanied by his or her boss, the overall impact can be highly therapeutic since we begin to realise that we are not alone and that our problems are equally shared by others. This, in itself, is no mean benefit and can bring a sense of proportion into careworn lives. Whether people remember the messages as well as the jokes is, of course, highly debatable. But even a temporary relaxation of stress is better than no relaxation at all.

Then there are those open days run by various management colleges to inform executives of their range of services. These are simply low-key marketing presentations, aimed primarily at impressing big-company personnel chiefs with endless reserves of potential MBAs. Impeccably organised and graciously hosted, they provide a welcome contrast to the more aggressive tactics employed by many commercial trainers (indeed, the staff would be scandalised if accused of 'selling'). However, a difficulty that soon emerges during the presentations is the length and cost of so many of the courses – which tends to put them beyond the reach of most smaller concerns. Another albatross that hovers over these academic wine-tastings is the question of the 'credibility' of the teaching staff, though much of the criticism is blatantly unfair. Nevertheless, it takes only one jargon-ridden talk by a mumbling 'behaviourist' to cause these prejudices to ignite anew.

There is one kind of meeting that you will have no choice but to attend; the good old company management conference, that annual excuse for riotous living amid the plush surroundings of a four-star hotel. Here, for a few carefree days, you can bask in the sunshine of a glowing future as new products are unveiled which – according to the chairman – will smite the competition hip and thigh. True, you may have heard it all before, but this is no occasion for parading your scepticism: it is a time for belief; nay, for soaring optimism. So stifle your reservations and keep on cheering. After all, if the Board can believe in miracles, why can't you?

CHAPTER EIGHTEEN

HOW TO AVOID MAKING THE WRONG SORT OF SPEECH

– RULE –

Learn the skills of effective speaking – many people judge a book by its cover.

I n the fantasy world of management literature, 'effective executives' always win. Armed with the latest management techniques (sanctified by the Harvard Business School), they rout the forces of autocracy and inertia like a computerized version of Robin Hood. Exuding initiative, chock-full of drive, they effortlessly climb the executive tree, pausing only to lop off the occasional branch that is luckless enough to be barring their path. Achieving their goals, they peer down at the ground and wave to the adoring throng below. Another victory for 'scientific management'! Merit and virtue have triumphed again!

So much for fairy tales, now for reality (a scarce commodity in most business schools). Far from being the kind of race that can only be won by the truly talented, business success is a many splintered thing in which chance and opportunism (those fleet-footed stallions) can often outdistance mere merit and energy. The glittering prizes do not always go to those with the most impressive records of achievement. They can just as easily go to those who have managed to shine at strategic moments.

This is why it is so tremendously important to learn the arts of effective speaking and acquit yourself nobly when opportunity knocks. If you are speaking at a meeting attended by top executives, it is vital to make the kind of impact that will be recalled with pleasure instead of shuddering horror. There are a number of strategies from which you can choose, but not all of them are equally effective. Some indeed are so fraught with peril that they can only be regarded as passports to oblivion.

BLOCKBUSTER

As its name suggests, Blockbuster is a muscular, aggressive type of oratory which should only be attempted by the ultra-confident since the dividing line between eloquence and megalomania can all too often appear perilously thin.

The main virtue of this style is that it can stun an audience into terrified submission, thus reducing the likelihood of awkward questions. With flailing arms and fortissimo delivery, speakers work themselves up into a kind of frenzy, casting a spell over their half-deafened audiences like a boa-constrictor hypnotizing a rabbit. Needless to say, Blockbuster requires both powerful lungs and a high degree of physical fitness. It is no use making the rafters ring if you suddenly collapse like a pricked balloon.

Many Americans love this barnstorming style: it reminds them of those religious revivals that sweep the States about every ten years. British audiences, however, can be a harder nut to crack since unless you are known as an out-and-out extrovert, the sudden adoption of this foghorn approach can arouse serious doubts as to your mental stability. It is pointless to exhaust yourself in thunderclap oratory if those listening believe that you have gone off your head. So beware of using Blockbuster in those pukka British companies where a speaker is expected to mumble, not shout.

JEREMIAH

This is a very popular style in British companies since it fits in perfectly with the national penchant for gloomy introspection and self-flagellation. Jeremiah-type speakers seek to project themselves as plucky triers whose dogged efforts have been thwarted by unfriendly gods. With much hopeless shrugging and upward rolling of the eyes, they tell heart-rending tales of lost production and cancelled orders, of late deliveries and wildcat strikes. True to form, they often arrive late for the meeting, their cars having broken down in heavy traffic.

'If only' is generally the Jeremiah's main theme. If only workers would work, if only customers would be patient, if only trade unions would be sweetly reasonable, what miracles of efficiency could they not perform! While cynics might regard them simply as buck-passers, their presentations are invariably well received since, being long accustomed to losing gracefully (whether in export markets or at sporting events), the British are unquestionably psychologically hardened to accepting defeats with quite incredible calm. 'There but for the grace of God go I,' is uppermost in many listeners' minds. 'No point in questioning this poor devil. That kind of luck could have happened to anyone.'

Jeremiah, however, is a strictly British technique and can be disastrous if used in foreign-owned companies, especially if parent-company executives are present. Americans, for example, want results, not excuses; Germans are, quite properly, impatient of inefficiency; and even the otherwise good-natured Dutch will be distinctly unforgiving if money has been wasted. Remember, sympathy for the bumbling amateur is a peculiarly British phenomenon. Many other nationalities are far less tolerant.

KITCHEN SINK

You can inspire an audience, enlist its sympathy or drive it to distraction with pettifogging detail. If you favour the third approach, you are a paid-up member of the Kitchen Sink brigade, those intrepid jugglers with charts and statistics for whom every molehill is a potential mountain. With their mind-numbing ratios and multi-coloured graphs, Kitchen Sinkers are the least attractive of speakers, mere podium pedants with minds like slide rules. When they rise to speak there is an audible sigh. The audience knows that it is time to sleep.

While Kitchen Sinkers are found in every function, the majority flourish in the quantitative disciplines such as accounting, engineering and operations research. Since even birds of their own feather can barely understand them, they should never be invited to speak at conferences where most of the audience are either no-nonsense salesmen or cynical marketeers who respect only 'flair'. It is hard to imagine more lack-lustre performers than the more dedicated exponents of Kitchen Sink. 'When in doubt, include everything' is their dreary motto. They are about as pleasant to listen to as a pneumatic drill.

Not surprisingly, since they drown their listeners in a sea of figures, it is rare for Kitchen Sinkers to be asked many questions lest they be tempted to prolong the agony still further (thus possibly endangering the pre-lunch drinking period). So if you have skeletons in your cupboard that you do not wish to be disturbed, you could do worse than consider this deadly technique. It will assuredly give you an 'easy ride' and you will at least be popular with the company alcoholics.

MACHINE GUN

For many executives speaking in public is a terrifying ordeal, a nerve-racking plunge into shark-filled waters. Even individuals who normally brim with self-confidence can suddenly be reduced to whey-faced zombies with tiny voices and trembling hands. It is as though they were crossing an uncharted minefield where every step could be their last. Consumed as they are with chronic nervousness, they seek only to 'get it over with' as quickly as possible.

And so, inevitably, disaster strikes. Clutching the microphone like drowning matelots and staring fixedly at their voluminous notes, they spray their audiences with verbal bullets like gangsters firing from a passing car. As these torrents of words engulf the audience the usual countermeasures begin to be taken. Posteriors wriggle, chairs scrape, and outbreaks of coughing fill the room. Unperturbed, the Machine Gunner carries on firing. Only another ten pages and it will all be over.

Such presenters have only themselves to blame if the audience takes cover instead of listening. They have yet to learn that most basic of rules: speakers must make themselves easy to listen to – it is for them to lead so that the group *willingly* follows. Many people will run for a stationary bus but *not* if it begins to accelerate away from them. Why make such an effort when the timetable shows that there will be another one along in just a few minutes?

RAMBLER

Whereas Machine Gunners are quivering jellies of nervousness, Ramblers are the most relaxed of speakers, treating the audience as though they were couriers pointing out the sights to a coachload of tourists. As they meander through their ill-prepared talks, pausing to explore every trivial issue, they give the impression that they are chatting to friends rather than attempting to communicate a serious message. Needless to say, this buttonholing style is deeply annoying to those who resent their time being wasted. Far from relaxing them, it merely irritates. Is the speaker, they wonder, becoming prematurely senile?

All this is lost upon the bumbling Ramblers who are under the impression that they are being well received. Oblivious of the chairperson's pleading gaze and still more of the fact that they have run out of time, they lumber towards their low-key finales as though reluctant to break up such a happy party. When finally they sit down they mistake the audience's sigh of relief for disappointment that the talk should have had to end. Beaming with pleasure, they stretch their legs and in a few moments are fast asleep.

Rambler is a technique that it is only safe to practise if you are a chief executive or are about to retire. While it has its uses on social occasions, it is totally unsuitable for business meetings which (in theory at least) have a serious purpose. Once you become known as a rambling bore everyone's ears will be closed against you. The only thing that will matter to the audience is how long it will take before you resume your seat.

PATRIOT

If you are deeply in love with both your job and your company (or are anxious to impress a visiting VIP), it could well repay you to use this technique, however great the cost to your self-respect. 'Patriot' tends to go down particularly well in those firms with outsize corporate egos which demand absolute obedience from their luckless executives. If 'theirs not to reason why' is the first rule of survival, then why not turn it to your own advantage?

Patriots are out-and-out company people who never miss an opportunity to declare their loyalty. Their speeches are littered with ref-

129

erences to 'this great company' and to the 'tremendous future' await-
ing 'our exciting new products'. It is rather like listening to a television commercial being performed by a particularly unconvincing
actor. The harder they try the more ludicrous they appear – at least
to those executives who have retained their sanity.

Nevertheless, if the company climate encourages such sycophancy
(many multinational companies fall into this category), then by all
means wave the flag whenever possible – it could pay off handsomely
in your next salary increase. No one will reproach you for ingratiating
yourself if such jingoistic fervour is merely par for the course. You
will simply be regarded as a loyal employee for whom an early
coronary would be a badge of honour.

HANGDOG

This technique has certain similarities with Jeremiah in that it seeks
to elicit sympathy for speakers and their problems. But whereas
Jeremiah can often be used successfully to put across a plausible
'hard luck' story, Hangdog is doomed to failure from the start since
it creates an impression of sheer incompetence. Hangdog people are
the kind who would have found the plagues of Egypt a blessed relief.
Stumbling through their various tales of woe, they flounder like
bathers who are out of their depth.

Essentially, they defeat themselves with their general aura of hope-
lessness. Apologising continually for losing their notes, voices drop-
ping constantly to a depressing whine, they envelop their listeners
in a pall of gloom from which it would seem there is no escape.
Invariably they are as inept as speakers as they are at solving their
real-life problems – and, if anything, are even more accident-prone.
Hand them a glass of water and they are sure to spill it. Any
equipment they use is bound to break down.

However great your misfortunes and ill-starred your luck, never use
the Hangdog technique as a cure for your ills: the remedy is even
worse than the disease. It is better by far to admit your shortcomings
than to take refuge in complex explanations that suggest you have
been the victim of a vicious conspiracy – when you have simply been
blundering from pillar to post. Don't wait for your sins to find you
out. Admit them boldly and salvage what respect you can.

There are times in the lives of virtually all executives when they must learn to endure the spotlight's glare. And however much they may dislike having to 'put on a show' and exposing themselves to public scrutiny, it is vital that they learn how to grasp the nettle so that the experience, though taxing, is not unduly painful. Unfair though it may seem, managers are sometimes judged by their utterances as much as by their deeds. The race goes to the articulate, not to the tongue-tied. Whether we like it or not, we are all salespersons now.

CHAPTER NINETEEN

HOW TO BE A SOCIAL SUCCESS

– RULE –

Tread warily at social functions – the ice may be thin and the waters deep.

Ll work and no play makes Jack or Jill a dull executive – a point well understood by most senior managers (hence the profusion of week-end mariners and of grim-faced aspirants to a hole-in-one). Yet there are many occasions in business when what may seem like a setting for relaxed conversation is in fact a test of your executive skills – one which you cannot afford to fail. It is no use performing like a Hercules in the office if you are unable to cope with social events. The successful manager is a good all-rounder, not simply the master of a single craft.

COCKTAIL PARTIES

Absurd though it may seem, you can often do more to advance your career amid the superficial chatter of a cocktail party than through a lifetime's labouring in the executive vineyard. After all, many cocktail parties are given in honour of 'visiting firemen' – often top head-office executives – who are intent upon demonstrating to the lower orders that they want to be treated as 'one of the crowd'. The stage is set, therefore, for those frenzied exchanges of timeworn anecdotes that form the staple diet of these tiresome affairs. Your best defence against the more boring raconteurs is a sizeable intake of vodka martinis.

Nevertheless, it is not enough just to swallow your drink and bear it: you must also know where your duty lies. If it should fall to you to 'look after' the Great Ones, you must do your utmost to protect their vanity while at the same time ensuring that they meet the right people. Naturally, you will try to steer them well clear of any of those notorious 'axe grinders' who may seize the opportunity to tout their wares. Remember that although a VIP's mood may appear benevolent it could quickly change should he or she begin to feel bored.

If you can combine a Maigret-like shrewdness with the imperturbability of a Jeeves, the party is sure to be a resounding success. Give your guests every chance to shine by surrounding them constantly with professional sycophants who can be relied upon to laugh at their feeblest quips. Keep their glasses refilled and their egos appeased (the occasional 'sir' or 'ma'am' will be well received) and you will assuredly do yourself a power of good. It is no accident that many aides to successful generals often end up as generals themselves. They have said the right things and done the right things. What more could any autocrat ask?

EATING OUT

From time to time almost every senior manager has to play host to either top company executives or important customers: such expense-account junketings are part of the game. Nevertheless, informal and friendly though the atmosphere may be, it is all too easy to commit some horrendous gaffe which will quickly earn you the wrong sort of publicity. What you had hoped would be a memorable evening may end in the kind of tight-lipped embarrassment that may permanently scar your future relations. It is such incidents that shatter promotion dreams and cause executives to be exiled to managerial Siberias.

Obviously the better that you know your guests the easier it will be to suit their tastes. Here, however, are a few ground rules that may come in useful. Firstly, if your guests are Americans, never take them to one of those dimly lit bistros where all the waiters are exuberant extroverts: they may find such panache a little overwhelming. Generally speaking, American businessmen greatly prefer the wide open spaces of those chain hotel restaurants where the service is provided by humourless zombies and the menu is the same from Brussels to

Bangkok. Only when they are surrounded by their own kith and kin can most US executives truly relax. Preferring high technology to haute cuisine, even a handwritten bill tends to alarm them.

If, however, your guests are British, then they will be most appreciative of 'a touch of class,' i.e. an ambience that reeks of genteel refinement. The Edwardian decor, the portraits on the walls, the polished deference of the head waiter – these are the factors that really count: the quality of the food is a relatively minor consideration. Not so the Europeans, particularly the French and the even more demanding Italians. Whereas the average Englishman or woman will accept uncomplainingly the most execrable fare (having been conditioned by long years of stodge-eating at their public schools), Italians will regard such food as a personal affront and will vociferously and aggressively make their views known. Moreover, the typical British restaurant's strategy for dealing with customer complaints – a well-tried mixture of hauteur and indifference – is only likely to make matters worse. So play it safe and stick to those dimly lit bistros where they seem to *enjoy* a good shouting match.

DINNER PARTIES

Giving a dinner party in the privacy of your home is a particularly nerve-racking form of hospitality which requires careful planning if it is to succeed. You are, in effect, exposing your lifestyle to public scrutiny and inviting your guest to make all kinds of judgements about the sort of person that you really are. It is your personal tastes and standards that are basically on trial, be it your choice of wines or your spouse's conversation. As a person chooses, so he or she *is*. Often a bookcase can tell you more than a psychological test.

But the success of such an evening does not depend primarily upon the food and drink provided: an agreeable atmosphere is far more important. This raises, in turn, the vital question of which other guests should be invited to the party since this is where the main pitfalls lie. The key factor that should govern your deliberations is the temperament and interests of the business VIP. If he or she is conservative in both dress and morals, then do not invite some male exhibitionist who delights in talking about his transvestite friends. Similarly, delete from consideration any of your circle who are (a) left-wing activists, (b) DIY fanatics, or (c) visibly terrified of their domineering partners. Most important of all, never invite any of

135

those lofty academics for whom all businessmen are untutored peasants with an insatiable lust for material possessions. He or she will probably spend the evening talking about some obscure modern poet who, having refused to yield to 'the temptations of commercialism', died in poverty in his early twenties – not the cheeriest of topics over the walnuts and wine.

The safest people to invite are such solid bourgeois figures as doctors, solicitors and accountants – practical people with sensible partners and few delusions of intellectual grandeur. True, the conversation may not rise to Olympian heights, but neither are you ever likely to be embarrassed. After all, the object of the exercise is to have a nice, cosy evening, not to provide a battleground for conflicting ideologies. Let the academics have their poets and the revolutionaries their dreams. A discussion on tax havens can be far more rewarding.

COOK'S TOURS

Occasionally you may find yourself acting as a guide to some important visitors – buyers perhaps, or senior government officials whose goodwill is vital to your company's interests. Organising such a visit and ensuring that it goes smoothly requires careful forethought and meticulous planning: it is fatal to assume that 'it will be all right on the night'. Remember, it can take only a few minutes to destroy a relationship that may have been forged by a decade of diplomacy. One false move and you could find yourself branded as 'the birdbrain who lost us the Boggins account'.

Factory visits, in particular, pose a whole complex of problems: there are so many things that can so easily go wrong. Think, for example, of the effect upon a cost-conscious customer of witnessing groups of workers nonchalantly playing cards while they await the repair of their near-obsolete machines. Or of the sight of whole mountains of scrap rotting away in dingy backyards. Or of choked gangways, unguarded machines, and scruffy canteens with their flyblown pastries. Unhappily, these are everyday phenomena in all too many factories and can undermine confidence in a company's efficiency. If you allow such dirty linen to be exhibited in public you ought not to be surprised when orders are lost.

Be ruthless. Well in advance of the VIP visit brief local management on the standards that you are expecting and designate those who will be held accountable. Accept no excuses, reject all hard-luck stories and crack down hard on any professional pessimists who claim that you are asking them to do the impossible. Never hesitate to use such draconian methods if you detect any signs of complacency or indifference. An Augean stable is not cleaned up by kindness; it can take a little muscle power to get results.

CHAIRING CONFERENCES

Many large companies hold annual conferences of their senior managements; in others there are regular divisional meetings which are often attended by members of the board. Being selected to chair such an important gathering is a feather in the cap of the executive concerned, but it is all too easy for a copybook to be blotted and for prospects of advancement to be put at risk. It is no use bounding eagerly into the spotlight's glare only to fluff your lines and miss your cues. Few audiences will forgive such blatant amateurism and a management audience is no exception.

To be a good chairperson you need the patience of Job, the diplomacy of a UN secretary-general and the cunning of a renaissance prince. You must be capable of sitting through even the most inept presentation with an expression that suggests it is an oration of genius (even though the audience may be half asleep). You must know how to intervene when a discussion becomes heated and how to lower the temperature with a touch of humour. Most important of all, you must learn how to deal with those towering bores who are totally incapable of keeping to the point and whose maunderings can wreck a crowded agenda. The technique involved is simple but effective. You merely wait until they pause for breath, then break in and thank them for their contributions which you are sure 'have given us a lot to think about'. Then either call the next speaker or close the discussion. Silent waves of approval will break all around you.

The social side of the conference must also run smoothly. If the meeting is being held in a hotel, then make sure that the service is up to standard. Should you receive any serious complaints, don't waste your time arguing with underlings – go straight to the manager and demand satisfaction. Sad to relate, such is the inertia of some British hotels that only aggressive behaviour seems to produce results. So cast off your inhibitions and start waving your arms. Nothing ever comes to he or she who waits.

HANDLING THE MEDIA

Unless you work in public relations you are unlikely to have had much contact with the media. Nevertheless, incidents can happen in any company as a result of which you may find yourself being interviewed by reporters and perhaps even appearing on radio and television. No matter how brief the interview may be, your message will be reaching a far wider audience than any which you could hope to command in business. Like it or not, you are your company's ambassador, and it is vital that you create a favourable impression.

Unfortunately, many executives perform abysmally during these interviews. Tight-lipped, wooden-faced and grotesquely over-cautious, they behave like people who have something to hide, even though this may be far from the case. They make little attempt to sell either the company's point of view or their own personalities and constantly allow themselves to be put on the defensive. Amazingly enough, men and women who think nothing of making strategic decisions that critically influence their companies' futures often visibly wilt under aggressive questioning and leave an impression of bumbling incompetence.

There are three golden rules for handling the media: know your facts, answer briefly and look and sound *enthusiastic*. As regards facts, remember that it is better to punch home one or two key points than to fire off a dozen at machine-gun speed. Keep your answers brief and to the point – don't pad them out with unnecessary verbiage. Finally, be *animated*: a touch of theatricality will add conviction to your case. After all, if you sound thoroughly weary of the whole affair, you can hardly expect to win much support elsewhere. There is nothing undignified about showing enthusiasm. It is the best possible way of conveying sincerity.

However much you may be needled during the interview, resist the temptation to blow your top. You can be commanding without being rude and it is foolish to show resentment at being asked tough questions. The interviewer's job is to get you to come alive – to encourage you to behave like your normal self. The more you help to achieve that objective, the more likely you are to achieve your own.

One final point. Even the most sure-footed executive must sometimes expect to meet his or her Waterloo: you cannot hope to win them all. There will be times, for example, when even the most carefully planned dinner party will end in disaster; when nothing will go right during a factory visit; and when, in spite of your crystal-clear statement to the press, you will still find yourself being misquoted. The only thing to do at moments like these is to recognise that things could hardly get worse and that your luck is bound to change for the better. After all, those whom the gods would favour they first put to the test. You ought not to resent it if they tease you occasionally.

CHAPTER TWENTY

HOW TO TUNE INTO PERSONNEL PEOPLE

– RULE –

Never make enemies in the Personnel Department – hell hath no fury like a eunuch scorned.

Rather like the harlot who attends Mass on Sundays but continues to ply her trade for the rest of the week, personnel experts find respectability elusive: they are among the least loved members of the management team. And not surprisingly, for their very existence is an affront to their managerial colleagues. After all, were most line executives deemed capable of recruiting good people, paying them fairly, and training them effectively, there would be no need for the services of these latter-day Solomons. Like housemaids employed by pampered matrons, their jobs are a tribute to their mistresses' lack of enthusiasm for tasks that they would rather abdicate to others. Not that personnel people are usually afflicted with any sense of gratitude. They are only too ready to pounce on line management's mistakes.

Nevertheless, if you are an ambitious executive with an eye to the future, you would be unwise to antagonise these lonely outcasts; they can be excellent guides through those executive quicksands which often engulf the unwary traveller. Light of step, skilled in bushcraft, they are skilled in the arts of self-preservation, accustomed to living by their wits in a jungle inhabited by far stronger predators. Capable of operating in a variety of terrains, they can usually be recognised by the following characteristics.

PEOPLE TRAPPERS

Armed with the business equivalent of bows and arrows – job descriptions and salary offers – the recruiters are the hunters of the personnel pack, lynx-eyed denizens of the most popular grazing grounds. Whether they are selling the company to gullible young graduates or overcoming the suspicions of seasoned executives, they are the arch-exponents of the glossy half-truth, weavers of dreams that fall just short of a promise. In their glittering world of make-believe futures, there are no dull jobs, only challenge and excitement; no disappointments, only lucrative promotions. Yet such is the magic of their fairy tales that many candidates believe them in spite of themselves.

Yet not every fish is so easily netted; some succeed in making their escape. This is nearly always due to the People Trappers' eloquence: their very smoothness is a danger signal to those who prefer a more robust approach. After all, those whose scepticism is still well honed are not likely to be satisfied by bland generalisations or by practised sidestepping of awkward questions. It is those candidates who are blinded by their own illusions who tend to fall victim to such polished wiles. But this, of course, is only to be expected. There is nothing easier to sell than hope.

But not all People Trappers are honey-tongued salespersons; some prefer a more mechanistic approach. There are those who put their faith in lengthy questionnaires that purport to tell all about a candidate's psyche, while others sing the praises of assorted tests with 'no right answers' (*then why ask the questions?*). The point about these 'selection aids' is that they can be used as scapegoats when errors are made. Should an unworthy recruit fall down on the job, his or her failure will be blamed upon 'faulty instruments' rather than the executive whose advice caused them to be used. This is why so many People Trappers are attracted to tests: they provide the perfect alibi for selection gaffes.

GAMESTERS

Of all the varieties of personnel experts, those whose trade is industrial relations are invariably the pacesetters in terms of sheer diligence. Day after day they spend long hours grappling with the fantasies of union negotiators or telephoning panic-stricken factory managers who are convinced that the world is about to end. After a few years on this endless treadmill, many deteriorate into cynical pragmatists who view their jobs as a kind of card game. If you can trump your opponent, all well and good; if not, then try not to lose your shirt.

While the best type of Gamester is a creative person who plays his or her cards with extraordinary skill, there are others who are simply glorified messengers between the union officials and company top management. Not surprisingly, the delays caused by this constant fetching and carrying (the unions, too, do their share of procrastinating) cause tempers to fray and disputes to escalate. And while there is much to be said for 'cooling-off periods' when both sides are deadlocked in a clash of principle, to build inertia into the bargaining process is to risk making a mountain out of every molehill.

Some Gamesters however, wily individuals that they are, do not resent these leisurely 'procedures' since they enable them to feign a kind of elder statesmanship that sets them apart from the lesser breeds. With worried frowns and bulging briefcases, they mutter incessantly of 'important issues' when usually all that is required is a pinch of common sense. But if you are a born appeaser with a horror of straight talking, then no wonder you are thought to have something to hide. Such ritual dances are not merely time wasting: they create a vested interest in the pursuit of trivia.

TORCH BEARERS

If you are going to appoint someone to train other people, then you had better make sure that he or she has something to offer: incompetent coaches do not produce champions. Yet, sad to relate, in all but the most enlightened organisations, the training department is a kind of terminal ward for failed executives from other disciplines. The result is that people who should be the torch bearers for new ideas are seen as managerial geriatrics, neo-pensioners who have retired from the fray. And indeed the atmosphere in some companies' training centres is as undemanding and restful as an old people's home.

But even when good people are selected as trainers, towering obstacles are often placed in their path – chiefly, the lack of management support. When the top persons themselves are so clearly illiterate on virtually any subject outside their own specialities – and are determined not to expose their ignorance – management training becomes a charade, a pointless exercise in make-believe. Not surprisingly, the trainers become increasingly dispirited and clamour to be transferred to other jobs. They have no wish to spend their lives playing games where both success and failure are greeted with indifference.

Some Torch Bearers, however, deserve to fail – not simply because of their lack of dynamism but because of their penchant for expensive 'training packages' which they use to conceal their own dearth of ideas. Companies that employ such individuals frequently find themselves spending considerable sums on a succession of specious wonder drugs, marketed by venal business consultants of quite unbelievable personal dreariness. And since most experienced managers know a 'rip-off' when they see one, it is hardly surprising that most of these packages are received in an atmosphere of icy hostility, broken only by the occasional cynical guffaw at the 'expert's' desecrations of the English language. Such persons as these have nothing to offer: they belong with the hucksters of downtown Las Vegas.

SURVEYORS

Considering the importance which most companies attach to money as a motivator, one would expect their salary specialists to be razor-sharp professionals, the very pick of the personnel crop. Not so. Far from being creative trail-blazers, many are merely overpaid clerks for whom original thinking is a distant relative. Content to preside over their mountainous records, recording the decisions that others have taken, these card-index emperors live stress-free lives, oblivious of the battles which rage around them.

True, they occasionally rouse themselves and participate in so-called 'salary surveys' (a questionnaire here, a few phone calls there) but the resultant data is of such dubious validity that it is rarely taken seriously by sceptical top management. What really counts in determining a company's salary policy is the advice that it receives from its financial experts and the settlements arrived at with the principal unions. Compared with the influence of either of these factors, the salary survey runs a very poor third. Frequently, it fails even to qualify for the race.

A company should pay what it has to pay in order to keep the people it needs – and sometimes it needs to be ahead of the pack. While this is well recognised by some large companies which operate in highly competitive environments, there are many more where the role of Surveyors is simply to confirm existing prejudices about what the salary pecking order ought to be. The result is that the firm's salary scales (if such exist) gradually lose touch with the realities of the marketplace and good performers are easily lured away. Only a radical approach can dispel such inertia, a mixture of intelligence and moral courage. A good Surveyor is worth his or her weight in gold; a plodder, by contrast, is merely excess baggage.

TRIMMERS

For personnel directors there is no middle way. Either they are a powerhouse of influence in the highest echelons, a major force for constructive change, or they are little more than their MD's poodles, ever anxious to carry out their master's bidding. If they are intelligent and courageous enough, they can be vital contributors to a firm's prosperity. But if they lack both vision and moral courage, they will be swept aside and virtually ignored.

The least effective personnel directors are undoubtedly the Trimmers; executives whose first (and only) concern is not to rock the management boat. Terrified of crossing swords with their fellow directors, they constantly yield to the strongest pressure, thereby forfeiting both credibility and respect. Desiring above all things to be loved by everyone, they pretend that the company is one big happy family where never is heard a controversial word. Afraid of making their own decisions, they spend most of their time in unnecessary meetings since they are strong believers in 'participative management', i.e. spreading the blame should things go wrong.

Sometimes, of course, the Trimmers are protected from the consequences of their inadequacies by the calibre and experience of those who work for them (they then become even more obvious figureheads). But this situation rarely lasts long as talented subordinates soon resent being used as human crutches for these blatant credit snatchers and 'vote with their feet' by joining other companies (unless they are locked in for personal reasons). The result is that the 'people department' becomes an object of ridicule and is widely regarded as being in need of the very remedies that it prescribes for

145

others. Not that this is likely to disturb the Trimmers. Good people for them are tiresomely argumentative; they much prefer the kind of heel-clicking conformists who, like themselves, find thinking difficult.

However, it is most important that you keep on good terms with your personnel people, whatever their calibre, since to fail to do so is to cut yourself off from a valuable source of 'inside information'. After all, a company is a veritable spider's web of communication networks, official and unofficial, sacred and profane, and no one sits nearer the centre of that web than those oft-maligned 'people people'. A word at the right time about changes in the pipeline can make all the difference between whether you are stormproof or are left floundering while the lifeboat pulls away for the shore. No survival-conscious manager ignores a warning beacon. Knowing where the rocks are can help to keep you afloat.

CHAPTER TWENTY–ONE

HOW TO IMPRESS VISITING AMERICANS

– RULE –

Never tell Americans that something is impossible – 'negative thinking' can be a capital crime.

I f you work for a subsidiary of a US multinational, then you had better learn fast how to handle Americans – a daunting but by no means impossible task. After all, if you aspire to greatness in such an environment, you must gain the confidence of those 'visiting firemen' who from time to time will visit your company to see how 'you fellas' are 'shaping up' and to scatter 'noo challenges' like visiting cards. But make no mistake: these roving ambassadors from the parent company can have a potent effect upon your future progress. Indeed, if you handle these visits clumsily, you may end up with no prospects at all.

Fortunately, Americans on the whole are not a devious people (at least not by conventional European standards), being far too concerned with wanting to be loved. But generous and charming as they undoubtedly are, they prefer to hear what they *expect* to hear and do not take kindly to implausible excuses. It is no use muttering about 'special problems' to men or women whose sole concern is with results. You must know how to make the correct responses and avoid being labelled 'a negative thinker'.

MAKING A FAVOURABLE IMPRESSION

Getting off on the right foot is all important: first impressions can make or mar your relationship. Being avid students of popular psychology, American executives are deeply sensitive to those telltale minutiae of personal behaviour which they have been taught to believe can be extremely revealing. A firm handshake, an upright posture, a level gaze: these are thought to indicate a competent executive. An individual who continually glances away is thought to have something dreadful to hide. So runs the folklore, cemented by countless inspirational books on leadership and by innumerable articles in the *Reader's Digest*. It is a simple creed and is none the worse for that. It gives its devotees a basic touchstone of 'character' and points the way to how a relationship may develop. The fact that the unexpected sometimes happens rarely deters the true believers. 'Sure,' they will agree, 'not *every* vice-president has a grip of steel. But doesn't the exception merely prove the rule?'

Be that as it may, you would be wise to conform to your visitor's expectations and to conduct yourself according to the unwritten codes. Above all, remember to *smile* – and keep on smiling. Many Americans believe that an unsmiling countenance betrays a disturbing coldness of heart ('if executives can't smile then how the hell can they lead?'). So ignore the strange looks that your subordinates may be giving you and let your face light up in your visitor's presence. There will be time enough to frown when the visit is over. The chances are that you will have good reason.

SAYING THE RIGHT THINGS

Most American executives believe that nothing is impossible and that one should never, *never* admit to defeat. Having fought a thousand mock battles at business school, they tend to see life as a series of case studies to which, of course, there are always tidy solutions. Ever optimistic and full of hope, they have little patience with gradualist approaches and believe that Rome would have been built in a day if only US contractors had been in charge.

So never talk to your visitors about 'insoluble' problems: it is asking them to renounce the American tradition of winning through against hopeless odds. Instead, outline whatever you have managed to accomplish and state what your plans for the next phase are. Do not antagonize them with references to 'cultural differences': as far as *they* are concerned it is a question of willpower. After all, if something has worked in Toledo, Ohio, then why shouldn't it work in Birmingham, England?

In short, be cheerful, positive and forward-looking: these are the qualities they expect – and respect. No matter how simplistic their advice may be, receive it as though it were a blinding revelation, full of dazzling new insights and rapier-like flair. And whatever your reservations, neither voice them nor show them: yours is to praise not to reason why. Give them the satisfaction of having 'solved' your problem. If they *have* to impress someone, it might just as well be you.

ASKING THE RIGHT QUESTIONS

Being conscious that they represent the world's most powerful nation, American executives dislike frank criticism: they prefer to receive the homage that they believe to be their due. After all, given America's matchless record of economic progress, they see themselves as ambassadors of managerial efficiency, bringing enlightenment to their less fortunate brethren. Having neither a Shakespeare nor a Machiavelli in their cultural tradition, they are alarmed (and sometimes angered) by European 'cynicism' which they regard as inimical to profits and growth.

This is why it is so tremendously important that you ask the right questions – questions that display a positive attitude and reflect the values of the American way of life. Your starting point should be 'how can we make this thing work for us?' rather than 'these are the reasons why it won't work here'. Ask questions – and plenty of them – about costs and profitability and always seek evidence of the expected benefits. By being 'hard-nosed' and probing in a businesslike way, you will convince your visitor that you are a kindred spirit, an American in all things except for your accent. Even here you can show that you are learning the language by using words like 'hopefully' in every other sentence.

So cast off your jingoism and join the great club: think, feel and talk like an American. But recognise that at best you can only be a replica and listen with respect when the oracle speaks. It is just not true that flattery will get you nowhere. It will get you a great deal further than if you say what you think.

SELLING YOUR ACHIEVEMENTS

If you are ambitious to succeed in an American company, you will need to become skilled in selling your achievements – it can be fatal to hide your light under a bushel. Americans are a forceful, extrovert people who are not unduly constrained by natural modesty and like to meet someone who can 'run with the ball'. You will be judged in terms of how you present yourself, so use capital letters and avoid the small print.

This means that you must master the art of making good presentations, particularly in the setting of formal meetings. Be aggressive, forthright and above all optimistic (any disasters should be dismissed as 'temporary setbacks'). Make sure that you have really done your homework and use plenty of convincing-looking statistics. However spurious they may in fact be, they are unlikely to be challenged if you sound confident enough. The figures themselves are not all that important. What matters is whether you seem like a 'winner'.

Be sure to use masses of visual aids to enliven your talk and build up interest. Americans grow impatient with the spoken word and greatly prefer to look at pictures. So unless you can speak like a latter-day Cicero, bombard them with charts, graphs and transparencies (cartoons will be especially well received). If 'one picture is worth a thousand words' – as most Americans fervently believe – then give the customers what they really want. This is particularly important if you are not a good speaker. They will be too busy looking to hear what you say.

AVOIDING TABOO SUBJECTS

Respect the ground rules that apply to such visits and avoid 'sounding off' about your boss or your pay. American executives have strong views on 'loyalty' and do not take kindly to 'negative thinking'. They object to being used as political pawns and are particularly impatient of criticism of the company. What to you may seem to be constructive criticism to them may be tantamount to communist subversion.

Much the same factors apply if you are discussing world affairs: even the most well-intentioned criticisms may be ill received. Believing that he who pays the piper ought to call the tune, Americans resent being treated as 'bumpkins' and 'fall guys' by 'smart-ass intellectuals' who can only sneer. So steer well clear of any controversial issues. Remember, unlike the British, Americans have no tradition of self-denigration. They believe that those who shout the loudest get the most attention.

However, there is no reason why you should not discuss your prospects with your visitor or how you feel about your current job: indeed, he or she may raise the subject first. And so long as you do not appear to be 'pointing the gun' at the company, you may well receive a sympathetic hearing – especially if you murmur about needing a fresh challenge. For of all the words in the US executive's vocabulary, 'challenge' is the one that is most 'OK'. It conjures up visions of dynamism and flair that go right to the heart of The American Dream.

BEING A GOOD HOST

As any executive who has visited the States knows, Americans are the most generous and warm-hearted of people who delight in entertaining their foreign guests. And by the same token they *expect* to be entertained during their frequent trips to the corporate outposts: what is sauce for the goose is sauce for the eagle. Being inveterate sightseers and camera buffs, they love to be taken on conducted tours where they can 'gee' and 'whizz' at the places of interest. So dust off your guide books and learn to be a good courier. There is no better way of selling yourself.

Wining and dining pose more difficult problems and it is important that you find out about your visitor's tastes. Contrary to their somewhat rumbustious public image, American male executives can be surprisingly puritanical and will not necessarily thank you for being bundled into the nearest strip club. Nor should you assume that they will *only* feel at home amid the transatlantic trappings of luxury hotels. Some may have had more than their fill of such expensive watering-spots and will be far more impressed by an invitation to your home.

151

Inviting your visitor to dine with you at home can be a masterstroke – provided that you avoid the more glaring pitfalls. If you have a partner, the make-or-break factor is their temperament, for it is he or she, not you, who will set the tone of the evening. Basically, all that is required of your partner is a ready laugh and an ability to listen. But if your beloved has strong political views – particularly if they have a radical tinge – then you would be wise not to take such a pointless risk. While Americans are used to being dominated by their families, they welcome a break when travelling abroad.

FOLLOWING UP THE VISIT

Though you sigh with relief when the visit is over, do not neglect the vital last step: contact your visitors when they are back in the States. After all, having devoted so much time to ensuring their welfare, you might just as well try to nurture the relationship – such an investment could well pay off one day. Most really senior appointments in American companies require the approval of corporate headquarters and it is important to make certain that your name is remembered. It is no use being competent if you are virtually unknown to those who make such decisions.

So write to your visitors, not too frequently but often enough to keep your memory green. Tell them how your projects are developing and how tremendously useful you found their advice. Remind them of any comments they made that have since turned out to be amazingly accurate and praise them for their uncanny perceptiveness. You need not feel that you are overdoing it for it is in the nature of Americans to prefer hyperbole. They would much rather hear something shouted from the rooftops than have it so watered down that it makes little impact.

'Getting along' with Americans is not as easy as it seems and can test to the utmost your political skills. The fact that they speak English is an historical accident that has resulted in so many illusions and problems that one sometimes wishes they spoke Swahili. Proud of their nation and dedicated to business, US executives are a noble species who have much to offer their European colleagues, not least in their commitment to personal freedom. If they occasionally appear brash and unduly aggressive, it is because of their drive to get things done. And maybe this is no bad thing. Such people may wear out but they rarely rust out.

CHAPTER TWENTY–TWO

HOW TO PICK A COMPETENT SUCCESSOR

– RULE –

Pick people with drive – it's what bridges the gap between promise and performance.

'Who would replace you if you were run over by a bus?' is a question that has revitalised many a management seminar, causing even the most somnolent executives to wake from their reveries. It is, of course, a most disturbing question – one which wreaks havoc in the minds of those managers who give no thought to what tomorrow may bring. It is ironic that it should take the image of a murderous bus driver to make such people aware of their own mortality. They have yet to learn to face up to that great inescapable truth: even if the bus doesn't get you, the company pension plan will.

Of course, if you are a long way from retirement, you may choose to ignore such unsettling thoughts and concentrate your energies upon staying on the payroll. But think. Are you not being a little unambitious? Are you *really* content to stay where you are? Yet you can hardly expect to move on to higher things unless you have trained a competent successor. Why should the company worry about promoting *you* if all you can offer it is a replacement problem?

Be smart. Make it easy for yourself *and* the company. Look around your department for someone who could replace you and do your best to help him or her to win their spurs. But how do you recognise such budding talents among the contenders who jostle for your throne – and how can you identify those who are unworthy? After all, executives are judged not merely by their personal efforts but by the achievements of those whom they pick as their successors. By proving yourself a poor selector of people you can jeopardise your own promotion prospects. It is *essential* that you develop the Midas touch.

CARBON COPIES

While it is always flattering to superiors to find that their methods are being copied, there are some people who take imitation to extremes. Chief among these are the Carbon Copies, subordinates who are determined to win the boss's favour by reflecting every facet of his or her style. Whatever the boss decides upon is good enough for them. They have not the slightest intention of thinking for themselves.

The trouble is that a carbon copy is never as sharp as an original and to promote such persons is to stifle creativity. Once the boss's guiding hand has been removed from the tiller the chances are that they will go to pieces and prove incapable of dealing with any new situation. True, they will go on doing those things that their former superiors have taught them to do, but without the tiniest flicker of personal inspiration. All they know is that something worked for their predecessors – so why shouldn't they be equally lucky?

Lacking a management philosophy of their own, it will not be long before they begin to flounder. Just as their previous bosses are trying to grapple with their new responsibilities, they will be bombarded with phone calls and lengthy memoranda imploring their help with a succession of 'crises' which invariably turn out to be relative trivia. This is only part of the price which must be paid for promoting Carbon Copies: equally disastrous is their effect upon morale. It is no accident that the best people begin to think about leaving. There is nothing to be learned from those who have nothing to teach.

BUSY BEES

One of the most persistent of all business myths is that effective executives are always busy and have not time to stand and stare. This, of course, stems from an elementary confusion between *activity* and *results* – for some of the busiest managers are also the least effective. Nevertheless, the idea that it is virtuous to be constantly busy dies exceedingly hard in many companies. The casual genius is an object of suspicion.

The reason for the Busy Bees' high level of activity is that they are totally confused about their objectives. They are Don Quixotes who tilt at windmills, puppy dogs who chase everything in sight. Being unable to distinguish the wood from the trees, their lives are dominated by their in-trays and telephones. It never seems to occur to them that they ought to get their priorities right. As far as they are concerned all problems are equal: to discriminate between them would be grossly unfair.

To promote Busy Bees is to invite instant anarchy; they will squander their inheritances in a matter of months. While they may have their merits as willing work-horses, they are completely incapable of providing leadership and will soon be ignored by their disgruntled subordinates. They are the kind of people who are fated to drown in a whirlpool of problems which essentially they have created for themselves. Don't hand such a person the keys of your kingdom. His or her place is strictly *outside* the gates.

WHIZZ KIDS

These restless individuals have many of the qualities of the ideal leader but lack the most important: common sense. Cheerful, brash and ever optimistic, they live in a world where all things are possible, convinced that every mountain is a potential molehill. Not only will they not take 'no' for an answer, they will act as though it were an unqualified 'yes'. They have a boundless faith in their own abilities and are completely unaware that people find them insufferable.

Whether he or she is the person to fill your shoes largely depends upon how patient you are. Trying to mature such individuals can be a nerve-jangling business and extremely expensive in terms of your time. For you have not only to bring them down to earth by demonstrating the weaknesses in their various schemes, they must also be shown how they are perceived by others. In short, you must set about their *political* education – knowing that they are likely to be extremely slow learners. The difficulty is that they are totally egocentric. They believe that they are the only ones marching in step.

Nevertheless, it is worth persevering since for all their rough edges they have plenty of talent. They often respond best to an aggressive approach that has all the subtlety of a charging rhino. It is no use relying upon honeyed words as they are virtually incapable of taking a hint. You will only get through to them by being direct. Throw away that stiletto and use a sledgehammer.

INFORMERS

Some people are content to let their deeds speak for them; others, lacking deeds, are left only with words. Informers use words like a slow-acting poison which dulls the alertness of their intended victims, softening them up for those sly insinuations that are at once their trademark and their *raison d'être*. For them, business is a conspiracy, a perpetual scenario of plot and intrigue in which only he or she who gets in the first blow can hope to survive amid the general carnage.

They would like to be their superiors' eyes and ears, their *eminences grises* and trusted confidants. They see their superiors as well-placed simpletons whom they can easily manipulate to their own advantage, having gained their confidence by regaling them with gossip – most of which they have invented themselves. They are masters and mistresses of innuendo, purveyors of half-truths and persons for whom ethics are a childish superstition. Their one aim in life is to win the boss's trust in the hope of being rewarded for their apparent 'loyalty'.

Regardless of any virtues they may have (and sometimes they are more than adequate performers), never dream of promoting such people: to do so is simply to proclaim your naivety. Trusting no one, they are distrusted by everyone. You can hardly expect a wolf to look after your sheep.

CAVALIERS

A curiously male phenomenon, the Cavalier is a man of considerable natural ability but needs constantly pushing to achieve his objectives. At heart he is a rather idle fellow who looks upon work as a necessary evil that serves merely to finance his expensive weekends. A frequenter of nightclubs and expensive restaurants, he is equally devoted to women and golf. But to his wife, if he has one, he appears an affectionate, industrious partner. She only wishes that he did not always have to work so late.

His performance at work is characteristically uneven. One day he is enthusiastic and brimming with ideas, the next he is cynical and apathetic. One can never be sure what his reaction will be when he is asked to take on anything new. He is just as likely to jump at a challenge as he is to complain about being 'overworked'.

Despite his many pleasing personal qualities, the Cavalier is a poor promotion bet: he is far too unstable and inconsistent. A man who is so clearly at the mercy of his genes is scarcely suited to a strategic role. Only he can sort out his personality problems. Before he can advance he must first grow up.

SYCOPHANTS

Sycophants walk in fear – fear of making their own decisions. It is a miracle that they have survived so long since they are totally incapable of thinking for themselves. Master crawlers and professional flatterers, they owe their positions to one thing only: their unfailing ability to keep nodding their heads.

Nevertheless, there is method in their madness for they have long since realised a great psychological truth: people who agree with the boss are usually well thought of. For despite their protestations that they welcome criticism, far too many managers are easily upset by those who expose the weaknesses in their arguments. They would far rather hear that everything is 'fine'; having to think again can be extremely tedious.

Sycophants are like pilot fishes – they are always on the look-out for a protective shark. Having attached themselves to people who are 'going places', they are content to do their patron's bidding with never a thought for their own self-respect. No task is too trivial, no chore too demeaning for these humble masseurs of executive egos. Let those who will fight over principles. They are perfectly happy to sit on the fence.

Not only are such individuals *not* promotion material but they are often extremely fortunate to be on the payroll. Their survival is a tribute to the power of flattery, to their skill in exploiting human frailty. Far from considering them for higher things, you should have already earmarked them for demotion or transfer. Have no fear: they will land on their feet. There is never a shortage of insecure bosses.

TOUGHIES

Here are managers who are often regarded as mavericks, laws unto themselves and 'difficult to manage'. Their reputations spring from their mordant outspokenness, their conviction that rules are made to be questioned and that policies are anything but holy writ. Terse of manner but keen of brain they are heartily disliked by the company's bureaucrats to whom their abrasiveness poses a threat. Such people would far rather be left alone to manipulate their 'systems' instead of having to answer the Toughie's embarrassing questions. Dispensing platitudes is more to their taste.

Provided that you can improve their political footwork, Toughies are your strongest promotion prospects. They are not only fully committed to their work but they have the necessary strength of character to get things done. Unlike most of their rivals who are anything but dedicated, Toughies revel in overcoming obstacles; for them today's impossibility is tomorrow's routine. Adventurous yet pragmatic, they are never soured or crushed by temporary setbacks. They merely grit their teeth and try again.

Like all entrepreneurs they have their share of enemies since such demonic energy always exposes the slothful. It is here that they can benefit from a little personal coaching, the aim of which should be to make them more skilful at negotiating the rapids of organisational change. Besides learning to suffer fools gladly, they also need a much wider repertoire of political talents. There is, after all, no point in attacking if one's opponents can be coaxed into giving themselves up.

Picking your successor is one of those tasks that can highlight whether you are truly mature. If you believe that what is required is 'more of the same', then go ahead and choose the Carbon Copy – but do not be surprised if he or she turns out badly. Playing for safety can be a dangerous game in a world in which managers must be light on their feet and quick to react to changing scenarios. It is better to select someone who will take a risk. Where there is no vision the people perish.